The case for the Crown : in re the Wigtown martyrs proved to be myths versus Wodrow and Lord Macaulay, Patrick the Pedler and Principal Tulloch.

Mark Napier

The Making of Modern Law collection of legal archives constitutes a genuine revolution in historical legal research because it opens up a wealth of rare and previously inaccessible sources in legal, constitutional, administrative, political, cultural, intellectual, and social history. This unique collection consists of three extensive archives that provide insight into more than 300 years of American and British history. These collections include:

Legal Treatises, 1800-1926: over 20,000 legal treatises provide a comprehensive collection in legal history, business and economics, politics and government.

Trials, 1600-1926: nearly 10,000 titles reveal the drama of famous, infamous, and obscure courtroom cases in America and the British Empire across three centuries.

Primary Sources, 1620-1926: includes reports, statutes and regulations in American history, including early state codes, municipal ordinances, constitutional conventions and compilations, and law dictionaries.

These archives provide a unique research tool for tracking the development of our modern legal system and how it has affected our culture, government, business – nearly every aspect of our everyday life. For the first time, these high-quality digital scans of original works are available via print-on-demand, making them readily accessible to libraries, students, independent scholars, and readers of all ages.

The BiblioLife Network

This project was made possible in part by the BiblioLife Network (BLN), a project aimed at addressing some of the huge challenges facing book preservationists around the world. The BLN includes libraries, library networks, archives, subject matter experts, online communities and library service providers. We believe every book ever published should be available as a high-quality print reproduction; printed on-demand anywhere in the world. This insures the ongoing accessibility of the content and helps generate sustainable revenue for the libraries and organizations that work to preserve these important materials.

The following book is in the "public domain" and represents an authentic reproduction of the text as printed by the original publisher. While we have attempted to accurately maintain the integrity of the original work, there are sometimes problems with the original work or the micro-film from which the books were digitized. This can result in minor errors in reproduction. Possible imperfections include missing and blurred pages, poor pictures, markings and other reproduction issues beyond our control. Because this work is culturally important, we have made it available as part of our commitment to protecting, preserving, and promoting the world's literature.

GUIDE TO FOLD-OUTS MAPS and OVERSIZED IMAGES

The book you are reading was digitized from microfilm captured over the past thirty to forty years. Years after the creation of the original microfilm, the book was converted to digital files and made available in an online database.

In an online database, page images do not need to conform to the size restrictions found in a printed book. When converting these images back into a printed bound book, the page sizes are standardized in ways that maintain the detail of the original. For large images, such as fold-out maps, the original page image is split into two or more pages

Guidelines used to determine how to split the page image follows:

• Some images are split vertically; large images require vertical and horizontal splits.
• For horizontal splits, the content is split left to right.
• For vertical splits, the content is split from top to bottom.
• For both vertical and horizontal splits, the image is processed from top left to bottom right.

THE

CASE FOR THE CROWN

IN RE

THE WIGTOWN MARTYRS PROVED TO BE MYTHS

VERSUS

WODROW AND LORD MACAULAY,
PATRICK THE PEDLER AND PRINCIPAL TULLOCH.

BY MARK NAPIER,
SHERIFF OF DUMFRIESSHIRE

EX UNO DISCE OMNES

EDINBURGH:
EDMONSTON AND DOUGLAS;
LONDON. HAMILTON, ADAMS & CO
1863.

PRINTED BY JOHN HUGHES, THISTLE STREET, EDINBURGH

CONTENTS.

PART FIRST.

THE ROMANCE OF THE WIGTOWN MARTYRS PROVED TO BE FALSE.

PART SECOND.

CRITICAL EXAMINATION OF THE RISE AND PROGRESS OF THE FABULOUS ROMANCE OF THE WIGTOWN MARTYRS.

PREFACE.

WHETHER two obscure women were or were not executed for high treason in 1685, would be a trifling question to deal with elaborately and systematically, if the case of the WIG-TOWN MARTYRS went no deeper. But it lies at the root of that cancerous growth upon the History of Scotland, the Martyrology of the Covenant. Close research has led me to the conviction, that not a single individual was unjustly put to death, for rebellion, or high treason, in Scotland, by the Governments of the Restoration. Unless fanatical assertion be equivalent to truth and justice, there are no sufficient materials for a Martyrology of Scotland during that period. That which we have from Wodrow is a calumnious tissue of monstrous fables. It has poisoned the History of Scotland to an extent that is now, perhaps, irremediable. He has misled all our historians of mark, from David Hume to Lord Macaulay, who have blindly followed him, and lazily, or lovingly, submitted to his rubbish, without an attempt at investigation. And thus it is that the national character of Scotland has been defamed by a mock and mythical martyrology of the lowest stamp, and her soil desecrated by fanatical monuments, not to commemorate the martyrs, but to perpetuate the calumny. Fountainhall, the Whig counsel for the gallows-martyrs of the Restoration, would have laughed Wodrow's Martyrology to scorn. That great lawyer and judge ever stood in political opposition to Lauderdale

and Queensberry. Like all political oppositionists, he was sometimes unfair in his record of their acts, and not always wrong in
his judgment of their policy. But had he been Lord Advocate,
instead of Sir George Mackenzie, not a single martyr the less
would there have been among the people of Scotland. This is
abundantly proved by his private journals, which are both
voluminous and minute. A kind-hearted man, an exemplary
Christian, of unblemished life, and a consistent Whig withal, he
has not a word to say about the *persecutions* or *cruelties*, of the
Government he opposed, civil or military. On the contrary,
he scorned the false prophets of the Conventicles, who furnished
him with those miserable clients, and never speaks of them but
with contempt. The excited victims themselves he never, in a
single instance, records as unjustly executed, or entitled to the
sacred name of martyrs. He has elaborate notes on that subject which might have saved the History of England from the
puerile pathos of those virulent fables which Lord Macaulay
culled, *con amore*, from Wodrow without further inquiry. In
reference to his own martyrological clients, Fountainhall, among
other admirable observations on the subject, says,—" The cause
must be very commendable, and justly and clearly founded on
the word of God, e'er a man can be esteemed a *martyr* for
suffering in it. *Non pœna sed causa facit martyrem.* And a
martyr ought to have a clear cause, and a humble frame and
preparation of spirit, and a knowledge of what he dies for."
But what would Fountainhall have said of Wodrow's grand
Martyrology, which is made up not only of such *mock* martyrdoms, most falsely told, but of *mythical* martyrdoms, as
fabulous in point of fact, as they are calumnious in spirit?
Weeded of fable, calumny, and fanatical railing, Wodrow's
two folio volumes would vanish, or resolve into an appendix of public documents that contradict him. His calumnious
legend of the life and death of John Brown, whom he dubs

"the Christian Carrier," no longer exists as truth in history It may suit some still to pretend, that the legal execution, under martial law, of an obstinate outlawed rebel, who had deeply forfeited his life to the laws of his country, who was lurking in arms at the very time to join the foreign invader, and who was carrying treasonable papers, is all one with the unintelligible murder, and by Claverhouse with his own hand. of a peaceable and industrious peasant, walking blamelessly in the sight of God and man. But thanks to the crowning discovery of Claverhouse's own letter, that ridiculous calumny has been utterly extinguished, in the face of Lord Macaulay's vicious adoption of it. No future historian will ever repeat that story as it has been told over and over again for nearly a century and a half None can now point, with the finger of truth, to a single act in the whole career of the high-hearted hero of Killiecrankie, that gainsays his own noble defence of himself,—" I am as sorry to see a man die, even a Whig, as any of themselves. But when one dies *justly*, for his own faults, and may *save a hundred to fall in the like*, I have no scruple."

But another Wodrow blotch, corrupting the blood of Scottish history to its heart's core, had spread wider and deeper still. It seems that "Memorials of Dundee" have not quite succeeded in eradicating the *Wigtown martyrdom*. It may not be absolutely disproved, pronounces a leading English journal of letters, but the proofs have been "rudely shaken." It has occurred to myself as a positive duty to the intelligent public, not to leave such a question imperfectly illustrated in a voluminous and expensive work such as "Memorials of Dundee," (out of which the materials were being already filched by feeble pamphleteers), but to produce the exposition of it in a shape more tangible and complete. So I now sit down before this last stronghold of the Wodrow martyrology, and hope to leave it also in ruins.

The proofs will here be found more thoroughly digested, and more systematically arranged, than could well be done in "Memorials of Dundee." In searching for more light, more has been discovered, and still to the effect of destroying the pet martyrdom of the Kirk. I have paused long enough, and searched deep enough, to justify some confidence that no deeper researches are likely to restore the credit of this calumnious romance. Keen and angry have been the struggles in some quarters to do so. But the result (itself an argument against the truth of the martyrdom) as yet may be stated in three words,—scribbling, nibbling, and quibbling.

What sort of a martyrdom is that, which, during the lapse of nearly two centuries, has *never been proved*; and, when challenged as a falsehood at the end of that period, is admitted, by its keenest supporters, not to be proved yet, and seemingly to be incapable of proof? What sort of *a tradition*, or "general belief," is that, which arose not at the time, and was expressly and positively denied to be fact before 1722, when Wodrow published, and *still* "denied to be matter of fact," in 1727, when Walker wrote? Some may think it both unnecessary and rash to attempt to prove the *negative*, that these "Wigtown Martyrs" were *not drowned*. But such is the nature of covenanting calumny, that unless that negative be proved, the Wigtown monument, which, "like a tall bully, lifts its head and lies," will continue to lift its head and lie as loud as ever. With what success that usually difficult task of proving a negative has been accomplished in the following pages, I now leave to the judgment of the Public.

MARK NAPIER.

6 AINSLIE PLACE,
　10th *March* 1863.

PART FIRST.

THE ROMANCE OF THE WIGTOWN MARTYRS PROVED TO BE FALSE.

PART FIRST.

THE ROMANCE OF THE WIGTOWN MARTYRS PROVED TO BE FALSE

SECTION I

Lord Macaulay's version of the Wigtown Martyrdom incredible on the face of it.

BY way of justifying a calumny he could not prove, and which he condescends to borrow from a sect he despised—that James II. was a monster of inhumanity, and his government of Scotland "Tophet on earth"—Lord Macaulay tells this story in his History of England:—

"The *eleventh of May* (1685) was made remarkable by more than one great crime. On the same day two women, Margaret Maclachlan and Margaret Wilson—the former an aged widow, the latter a *maiden of eighteen*—suffered death for *their religion* in Wigtownshire They were offered their lives if they would consent to *abjure the cause* of the insurgent conventiclers, and to attend *the Episcopal worship*. They refused, and they were sentenced to be drowned They were carried to a spot which the Solway overflows twice a-day, and were *fastened to stakes* fixed in the sand between high and low water-mark. The *elder* sufferer was placed near to the advancing flood, *in the hope* that her last agonies might terrify the *younger* into submission *The sight was dreadful.* But the courage of the survivor was sustained by an enthusiasm as lofty as any that is recorded in martyrology She saw the sea draw nearer and nearer, but gave no sign of alarm. She prayed, and sang verses of psalms, till *the waves choked her voice*. After she had tasted the bitterness of death, she was, by a *cruel mercy, unbound,* and *restored to life.*

When she came to herself, pitying friends and neighbours implored her to yield '*Dear Margaret*, only say, *God save the King*!' The poor girl, true to her *stern theology*, gasped out, 'May God save him if it be God's will.' *Her friends crowded round* the presiding officer—'She has said it; *indeed, sir*, she has said it.' 'Will she take the abjuration?' he demanded. 'Never!' she exclaimed, 'I am Christ's, let me go!' and the waters closed over her for the last time."—(*Hist.* vol. iv., p. 77. *Latest edition.*)

It is now pretty well understood, at least by all who read history for other purposes than mere amusement, that when Lord Macaulay discourses after this fashion, his facts are apt to be fabulous. The truth is, as regards the period of history he is thus professing to illustrate, the mind of this great author, all accomplished and well stored as it was, had become sadly warped on the subject of imaginary cruelties perpetrated, and always upon the weakest, the most innocent, and the most Christian, by the governments of the Restoration. Closing his mind against the light of truth from all incongenial quarters, he delighted to exercise his facile pen in epitomizing his political anathemas with a terseness of invective natural to his domineering talent, and in the current form, and upon such incidental occasions, as might scarcely seem to justify the expectation of an array of proofs, or a frank and accurate disclosure of authorities. Indeed, he was utterly reckless of historical proofs when in such a mood. Thus, in his essay on Hallam's History, referring to the commencement of the Restoration, he says :—

"The Government *wanted a ruffian* to carry on the most atrocious system of misgovernment with which any nation was ever *cursed*, to *extirpate Presbyterianism* by fire and sword, by *the drowning of women*, by the frightful torture of the boot, and they found him among the chiefs of the rebellion, and the subscribers of the Covenant."

Of course, this means Lauderdale, who, as all the world knows, passed, by a transition easily accounted for, from his Presbyterian glory as a "prime Covenanter," to his more notorious career as a bloated courtier. But never a woman did Lauderdale drown, whatever other sins he may have to answer for. Was the fact really unknown to Lord Macaulay, that the *only* case ever specifically alleged by the bitterest and most unscrupulous of Covenanting pamphleteers in the very hey-day of the Revolution, of the drowning of any State criminal, male or female, from the restoration of King Charles to the crowning of King William, is this solitary mythical case of *Margaret Lauchlison* and *Margaret Wilson* in 1685? Unless that story be true, no woman whatever was executed by drowning *during the whole period of the Restoration.* And whether true or false. no woman whatever was so disposed of during the administration of Lauderdale, who died in 1682.

Then as for Lord Macaulay's version of this melo-dramatic martyrdom, what reflecting mind could peruse it and not be struck with the total absence of *vraisemblance* that pervades the whole narrative? Had such a story been told by Sir Walter Scott for the purpose of debasing the character of King William, Lord Macaulay would have been the first to visit it with the most withering scorn. Mark the evasion of all explicit historical elucidation, or proof, in a question of great historical importance. Could that *ad captandum* mode of telling such a story have any other object than to escape the test of historical investigation? Still, with all the art of his diction, the romance, as he gives it, seems improbable in the highest degree. Under what authority, judicial or executive, could it possibly have happened, that such a scene was enacted, hard by the royal burgh of Wigtown, as if wantonly to excite the feelings, inflame the passions, and strengthen the cause of the most rebellious population in Scotland, at the very time when Argyle's invasion was daily expected in that quarter? No such scene had ever occurred in Scotland before. No such scene has ever occurred in Scotland since Can there be discovered any Commission of Justiciary, or any order of Council in 1685, under which aged and young of the female sex. saintly in their lives, and harmless in their habits, could, by any possibility, have been " sentenced to be drowned " for declining " to attend the Episcopal worship?" And as for refusing " to *abjure the cause* of the insurgent Covenanters," what does that mean? If it mean, obstinately and violently, in the face of a tribunal of justice, and in presence of an audience of the people in a rebellious district, refusing to *disown,* and to absolve themselves, in terms of the Government test, from being connected with Renwick's anonymous pro-

clamation of war against the State, and his violent incentives
to assassinate the advisers and loyal adherents of the Crown,
paraded on all the church-doors and market-crosses in the
south and west of Scotland (and the *Abjuration Oath* of 1685
required no more), Lord Macaulay was guilty of *suppressio
veri* in not saying so. And had he ventured to be historically
explicit on the subject, the answer must have met him, that
these females, whose mythical fate he so elaborately, but
somewhat fantastically narrates, could not have been the para-
gons he figures, seeing it can be distinctly proved that they
were tried and condemned by Lords Commissioners of Justiciary, to whom the Privy Council had issued this precise,
peremptory, and humane direction,—"But at this time you
are not to examine *any women* but such as have been *active* in
the said courses *in a signal manner.*"

To all conversant with the history of Argyle's invasion in
1685, so alarming for the regal Government, and who are
well read in the records of the Privy Council of Scotland, it is
known that such Royal Commissioners were always placed
under the most precise official instructions, strictly defining
their duties, both as regards trial and punishment, instructions
beyond which they never presumed to act, and could only
have done so at their highest peril. Was there ever any such
direction as this, that if an aged matron and a young maiden
should happen to be tried and condemned together, "for their
religion," as Lord Macaulay has it, that they were to be
drowned by this very novel *modus operandi:*—The old one
was to be fastened to a stake driven into the sand of the making tide, nearer the devouring ocean than the stake provided
for her youthful partner, "that her last agonies might *terrify*
the younger into submission?" Was there any instruction or
authority whereby venerable Christianity, hallowed by age,
tried by long years, was, at the arbitrary fiat of some "presiding officer," to have no measure of mercy allowed, but was
destined to enact, after this very peculiar fashion, the part of
decoy-duck to "cruel mercy?" The details of Lord Macaulay's
episode are absolutely incredible, and all the embellishments
bear the stamp of the most fantastical invention. The story
runs (to adopt a favourite phrase of his own, certainly not

belonging to legitimate history), that the "maiden of eighteen" was not to be so seduced; that the tide of the terrible Solway came rolling on and "choked her voice" until she "tasted the bitterness of death," upon which she was "unbound and restored to life." What! with the tide of the Solway rushing over head? Was she tied to the stake by a slip-knot? She was restored, however, to life, to speech, and to loyalty, for she "gasped out" a most orthodox, though somewhat elaborate version of *God save the King.* The "presiding officer," and, pray, who was he? being a glutton in "cruel mercy," was not satisfied, however, and without a vestige of authority to assume that very important function, pressed the *Abjuration Oath* upon a condemned criminal, dead in the eye of the law, and more than half executed in point of fact! "'Never!' she exclaimed, 'I am Christ's, let me go!' and the waters closed over her for the last time." Did Lord Macaulay really believe this nonsense himself? By this time, unless the tide stood still, the stake must have been under water. How was this virgin sacrifice really consummated? Was she tied to the stake again, or did "cruel mercy" just cast her neck-and-crop into the water to sink or swim? On the part of *History proper,* common sense demands some explicit and intelligible statement as to the practical conclusion of this very extraordinary operation. We are not trifling: these are not carping or silly questions. We do not, indeed, profess to treat this sensation romance with the slightest respect. We have learnt to hold it in the greatest contempt. But here is a fair cross-examination of a highly responsible historian, under which, we suspect, Lord Macaulay would have found himself compelled to remain absolutely silent. But let us now confront him with his *sole authority*, which he only vouchsafes to give, at the foot of his page, in this very curt form—" *Wodrow*, III., ix., 6."

SECTION II.

Wodrow's version of the Wigtown Martyrdom ignored by Lord Macaulay in its most essential circumstances, while professing to found upon it.

The passage in Wodrow's " History of the Sufferings of the Church of Scotland," referred to by Lord Macaulay, occurs under this violent *ad captandum* title, which Wodrow had copied from Alexander Shield's " Hind Let Loose." " Of the *murders* in the fields ; the *barbarous drowning of women* within the sea-mark ; the *murder* of Polmadie and others, this 1685." Wodrow's sole illustration, indeed the *only* example adduced by *any chronicler whatever,* from that time to this, of the " drowning of women," during the whole reigns of the Restoration, we must here give entire, in the very words of the martyrologist :—

" Upon the 11th of May (1685), we meet with the *barbarous and wicked* execution of two *excellent* women near Wigtown, *Margaret M'Lauchlane* and *Margaret Wilson.* History scarce affords a parallel to this in all its circumstances ; and therefore I shall give it at the greater length ; and *the rather,* because the *advocates for the cruelty* of this period, and *our Jacobites,* have the *impudence* some of them to deny, and others to extenuate, this matter of fact, which can be fully evinced by many living witnesses And I shall mostly give my narrative of it, from an account I have from the forementioned Mr Rowan, now with the Lord, late minister of Penninghame, where Margaret Wilson lived, who was at pains to have its circumstances fully vouched by witnesses, *whose attestations are in my hands ;*[1] and I shall add, to make the account more full, the sufferings of the said Margaret's relations, though not unto death, as coming in natively enough here, and what will hand me in to what I have most in view.

" Gilbert Wilson, father to the said Margaret, lived in Glenvernoch, belonging to the laird of Castlestewart, in the parish of Penninghame, and shire of Wigtown, and was *every way conform to Episcopacy,* and his wife *without anything to be objected against her* as to her regularity. They were in good circumstances as to the world, and had a great stock upon good ground, and *therefore* were the fitter prey for the persecutors,

---

[1] The nature of Mr Rowan's communication to Wodrow, and the disingenuousness of the latter in pretending to possess " attestations by witnesses " of the martyrdom in question, will appear in the sequel.

if they could reach them. Their children, to be sure, not from their *education*, but a *better principle*, would by no means *conform*, or hear the Episcopal incumbent This was a *good handle* to the persecutors, so they were searched for, but fled to the *hills, bogs, and caves*, though they were yet scarce of the age that made them obnoxious to the law. Meanwhile their parents are charged, at their highest peril, not to harbour them, supply them, or speak to them, or see them, without *informing* against them, that they might be taken, and their father was fined for his *children's* alleged irregularities and *opinions*, which *he had no share in*, and harassed by frequent quarterings of the soldiers, sometimes a hundred of them upon him at once, who lived at discretion upon anything in the house or field belonging to him

" Those troubles continuing upon him for *some years together*, with his attendance upon courts at Wigtown, almost once a week, thirteen miles distant from his house, his *going to Edinburgh*, and other harassings, brought him under exceeding great losses At a modest calculation they were above five thousand merks ; and all for *no action or principle of his own*, for he was *entirely conformist*. He died some six or eight years ago in great poverty, though one of the most substantial countrymen in that county. And his wife (1711) lives, a very aged widow, upon the charity of friends. His son, Thomas Wilson, a youth of *sixteen years of age* this February 1685, was forced to the mountains, and continued *wandering* till the Revolution, at which time he went to the army, and bore arms under King William in Flanders, and after that in the Castle of Edinburgh. He never had a farthing from his parents to enter that ground which he possessed ; but having got together somewhat by his own industry, lives now in his father's room, and is *ready to attest all I am writing*.

" It is Gilbert's two daughters who fell into the hands of the persecutors—Margaret Wilson, of *eighteen* years of age, and Agnes Wilson, *a child not thirteen* years—that have led me to this account. Agnes, the youngest, *was condemned with her sister* by those *merciless* judges, but her father obtained a liberation from prison, under a bond of a hundred pounds sterling, to present her when called However, Gilbert had to *go to Edinburgh* before she was let out ; but to all *onlookers*, and *posterity*. it will remain an *unaccountable* thing, *to sentence a child of thirteen years to death*, for *not hearing*, and *not swearing* [1]

" In the beginning of this year (1685), those *two sisters* were obliged to abscond, and wander through Carrick, Galloway, and Nithsdale, with their brothers and some others After the universal severities slackened a little at King Charles's death, the *two sisters* ventured to go to Wigtown to see some of their suffering acquaintances there, particularly *Margaret M'Lauchlan*, of whom just now. When they came to Wigtown, there was an acquaintance of theirs, Patrick Stewart, whom they took to be a

---

[1] Wodrow here assumes, as an unquestionable fact, that which could not possibly have occurred, which he makes no attempt to prove, and then calls it " an unaccountable thing !" Of this afterwards.

friend and wellwisher; but he was really *not so*, and *betrayed them*
Being in their company, and *seeking* an occasion against them, he pro-
posed *drinking the King's health* This they *modestly declined;* upon
which he went out, informed against them, and brought in *a party of
soldiers*, and seized them As if they had been great malefactors, they
were *put in the thieves'* hole; and after they had been there some time,
they were removed to the prison where *Margaret M'Lauchlan* was,
whom I come next to give some account of.

" This woman was about sixty-three years of age, relict of John Mul-
ligen, carpenter, a tenant in the parish of Kirkinner, in the shire of Galloway, in the farm of Drumjargan, belonging to Colonel Vans of Barnbarroch She was a countrywoman of *more than ordinary knowledge,
discretion*, and *prudence*, and, for many years, of *singular piety and devotion*. She would take none of the oaths now *pressed upon women* as well
as men [1] Neither would she desist from the duties she took to be incumbent upon her, hearing Presbyterian ministers when Providence gave
opportunity, and joining with her Christian friends and acquaintances in
prayer, and supplying her relations and friends when in straights, though
persecuted. It is a jest to suppose her guilty of rising in arms and rebellion, though indeed it was a part of her indictment, which she got in
common form now used. For those great crimes, and no other, she was
seized some while ago, upon the Lord's-day, when at *family worship* in
her own house, which was now an *ordinary season* for apprehending
honest folk She was imprisoned, after she had suffered much in her
goods and crop before she was apprehended. In prison she was very
roughly dealt with, and had neither *fire*, nor *bed to lie upon*, and had very
little to live upon.

" Jointly with Margaret M'Lauchlan, or M'Lauchlson, these two
young sisters, after many methods were taken to *corrupt* them, and
make them swear the oath now imposed,[2] which they steadily refused,
were brought to their trial before the Laird of Lagg, Colonel David
Graham, sheriff, Major Windram, and Provost Cultrain, who gave *all
the three* an indictment for rebellion, Bothwell Bridge, Ayrds moss, and
being at twenty field conventicles. No matter how false and calumnious poor people's indictments were.[3] None of the pannels had ever been
within twenty miles of Bothwell or Ayrdsmoss. Agnes Wilson could be
but eight years of age at Ayrdsmoss; and her sister but about twelve or

[1] While telling this cock-and-bull story, every paragraph of which
bespeaks its falsity, Wodrow was perfectly cognisant of that order of the
Privy Council 1684-5, which says,—" But at this time you are *not to
examine any women*, but such as have been *active* in the said courses, *in a
signal manner*."

[2] The Abjuration Oath of 1684-5, of which afterwards.

[3] These are all gratuitous assumptions of Wodrow's own, as to the
contents of their indictment, of which there is no record extant, except a
notice of it in the old woman's petition for mercy, and which notice *completely contradicts* Wodrow's account, as will be seen afterwards.

thirteen ; and it was *impossible* they could have any access to those risings Margaret M'Lauchlan was as free as they were

" *All the three* refused the *Abjuration Oath*, and it was *unaccountable* it should be put to one of them.[1] The assize bring them in guilty, and the Judges pronounced their sentence, that, upon the 11th *instant* [May], *all the three* should be tied to stakes fixed within the flood-mark in the water of Blednoch, near Wigtown where the sea flows at high water, there to be drowned We *have seen* that *Agnes Wilson* was *got out* by her father upon a bond of an hundred pounds sterling, which, *I hear*, upon her *non-production*, was likewise exacted. *Margaret Wilson's* friends used all means to prevail with her to take the *Abjuration Oath*, and to engage to *hear the curates*, but she stood fast in her integrity, and would not be shaken. They received their sentence with a great deal of composure, and *cheerful countenances*, reckoning it their honour to suffer for Christ and his truth During her imprisonment *Margaret Wilson* wrote a large letter to her relations, full of a deep and affecting sense of God's love to her soul, and an entire resignation to the Lord's disposal She likewise added a vindication of her refusing to save her life by taking the *abjuration*, and engaging to conformity, against both she gives arguments with a *solidity of judgment* far above one of her years and education [2]

" This barbarous sentence was executed the foresaid day, May 11th, and the two women were brought from Wigtown, with a *numerous crowd of spectators*, to so *extraordinary* an execution Major Windram, with some soldiers, guarded them to the place of execution. The old woman's stake was a *good way in beyond* the other, in order to *terrify* the other to a compliance with such oaths and conditions as they required. But in vain ; for she adhered to her principles with an unshaken confidence When the water was overflowing her fellow-martyr, some about *Margaret Wilson* asked her what she thought of the other now struggling with the pangs of death? She answered,—' What do I see but Christ in one of his members, wrestling there. Think you that *we* are the sufferers? No ; it is Christ in us, for he sends none a warfare on their own charges ' When *Margaret Wilson* was at the stake she sang the 25th Psalm, from verse 7th downward a good way, and read the 8th

---

[1] It would indeed have been " unaccountable " had they offered it to a child " not *thirteen* years of age." The royal proclamation on the subject is thus noted by Fountainhall ·—

" *December* 30, 1684 —There is a proclamation at the market-cross of Edinburgh, ordaining an oath to be tendered to all *past sixteen years of age*, disclaiming the *declaration of war*, mentioned 13th November 1684, and the *assassination principles* of the lawfulness of murdering the King's soldiers ; and thereupon to have a *pass and certificate*, else to be reputed as favourers of them."—*Fountainhall's Decisions*, i. 328.

[2] This letter is not forthcoming in Wodrow's History, nor is it to be found among his manuscripts, or anywhere else Wodrow's statement, with regard to it, is copied *verbatim* from the " Cloud of Witnesses " Of this afterwards.

chapter of the Romans with a great deal of cheerfulness, and then prayed
While at prayer, the water *covered her*, but before she was quite dead,
they *pulled her up*, and held her out of the water till she was recovered,
and able to speak, and then, by Major Windram's orders, she was asked
if she would pray for the King? She answered, she wished the salvation
of all men, and the damnation of none One, deeply affected with the
death of the other, and her case, said,—' *Dear Margaret*, say *God save
the King*, say *God save the King*.' She answered, in the greatest steadi-
ness and composure, —*God save him*, if he will, for it is his salvation I
desire. Whereupon some of her *relations* near by, desirous to have her
life spared if possible, called out to Major Windram,'—'Sir, she hath said
it, she hath said it' Whereupon the Major came near, and *offered her
the abjuration*, charging her instantly to swear it, otherwise return to the
water. Most deliberately she refused, and said,—' I will not, I am one
of Christ's children, let me go.' Upon which she was *thrust down again*
into the water, where she finished her course with joy She died a
virgin martyr, about *eighteen* years of age, and both of them suffered
precisely upon refusing conformity, and the Abjuration Oath,[2] and were
evidently innocent of anything worthy of death, and since properly they
suffered upon refusing the *abjuration*, for refusing of which *multitudes*
were cut off in the fields with less ceremony, and at the time when these
murders were so common, I have brought them in here

" *It is of more importance to observe*, that, in the Council-Registers,
since I wrote what is above, I find what follows —' *April* last, *Margaret
' Wilson* and *Margaret M'Lauchlison*, under sentence of death pronounced
' by the Justices, are continued till   , and the Lords of his
' Majesty's Privy Council recommend it to the Secretaries to procure their
' remission ' The day to which they are reprieved is blank in the records;
but I may safely suppose it would be for a longer day than the 11th of
May, there being scarcely time, betwixt the 30th of *April* and that, to
get a return from the Secretaries. Indeed, at this time a recommendation from the Council for a remission was looked on as *a material pardon*;
and if I may *conjecture*, Gilbert Wilson, when he, *as we heard*, after the
sentence of *all the three*, made application at *Edinburgh*, seems to have
prevailed as to all the three, and the case was *extremely favourable*. If
matters stand thus, the *people at Wigtown* are deeply guilty, and had *no
powers* for what they did; and the death of these persons was what the
Council *ought to have prosecuted them for* "

Are we to laugh or cry? *Solventur risu tabulæ.* This
concluding information is indeed " of more importance " than
the whole tissue of wild improbabilities, and *impossibilities*,
which precedes it. So important is it, that had the truth and
justice of history been a principle of Wodrow's undertaking,

---

[1] Windram was only captain-lieutenant of dragoons
[2] It will be proved in the sequel that both of these women did take the
Abjuration Oath.

he would have drawn his pen through all that goes before, and, as to this martyrdom at least, commenced his researches anew. It fairly entitles the intelligent reader to do so. Even by his own shewing, the Government he so recklessly assails, instead of perpetrating this " unaccountable " cruelty, as he might well call it, had interposed *humanity*. These two women, instead of being executed in terms of their sentence,— under that grand melo-dramatic exhibition for which the genius of Lord Macaulay found the phrase " cruel mercy,"— were reprieved by the Privy Council in a form which even Wodrow confesses to be " a material pardon." And is that feeble conclusion all the martyrologist had to say about a discovery which, as we shall find, really turns the whole of his glaring improbabilities into an impossibility ? Was there ever so meagre a proportion of the *bread* of historical candour to so inordinate a measure of the *sack* of fanatical calumny ! That discovery, manifestly most unwelcome to the martyrologist, as it is even now to his disciples of the present day (whom we have only very recently compelled for the first time to face it), destroyed at once, as he must have seen, not merely the accusation against the Government, but one of the most salient and startling particulars that embellish his romance. He had the boldness to assert that a child " not thirteen years of age," a girl scarcely out of her infancy, had been capitally tried with the other two, received her sentence with a " cheerful countenance," and was in like manner condemned " to be tied to a stake fixed within the flood-mark, there to be drowned ! " He perils this monstrous assertion (unsupported, as usual, by a shadow of evidence), entirely oblivious of the fact that the royal proclamation, and orders of the Privy Council, by authority of which these two women had been brought to trial, were expressly limited, in the application, to parties *above the age of sixteen*. But his own subsequent discovery clinches that matter. This female child, he says, was condemned to death with the other two. But she is not *reprieved* along with them. Was it not as necessary to apply for the royal mercy in her case as in that of her elder companions ? If condemned to death in company with her adult sister, would she not have been reprieved along with her ? Do we require further evidence to satisfy us that *that* part of Wodrow's story, at least, is a falsehood as absurd as it is calumnious? Are we bound to be tender of it, and to give it a gentler name?

Then, it will be observed, Wodrow had premised his verbose romance with an indignant announcement, that, at the time he is writing, between 1710 and 1722, a very large proportion of the intelligent community, whom, *more solito*, he strives to disparage by the odious epithets, " the *advocates* for the *cruelty* of this period, and *our Jacobites,*" actually *denied the truth* of this drowning story altogether. And yet, after all his hectoring on the subject, he is constrained to wind up with so complete a justification of the very denial he had denounced as "impudence," that, verily, "our Jacobites" of 1710-22 required no further justification.

And what does Lord Macaulay make of all this? Is it not deplorable—does it not rouse the indignation of every just mind, and clear understanding—to find an author of his great powers, and high position, pandering to, and even going beyond, the historical calumnies of Wodrow, instead of detecting and exposing them? Must we be tender of that too? Can we treat his own pretensions, as a great historian, with perfect respect, when we find him, so dictatorially, and in the most unqualified terms, recording the execution of these two women as an act of the most *savage cruelty* on the part of *James II.;* giving the illustration expressly in reference to his violent assertion, that, " the *fiery persecution* which had *raged* when James ruled Scotland as Viceroy, waxed *hotter than ever* from the day on which he became Sovereign ; " and, in support of all this, vouchsafing no other reference than " *Wodrow,* III., ix. 6; " there being under Lord Macaulay's eye at the very time, in the very page he is quoting, Wodrow's own most important admission, that, after all the calumny he had penned, the fact had unexpectedly risen up, in judgment against his reckless history, that these two female martyrs had actually been reprieved by the Privy Council, and reprieved in a form he is constrained to admit amounts to " a material pardon ; " that " the case was extremely favourable ; " that he, Wodrow, was thus driven to " conjecture " that the application for mercy had "*prevailed* as to *all three*," and that it must have been some *unauthorised murderers*, whom he blindly designates as "the people at Wigtown," who had put the women thus publicly and dramatically to death, in defiance of the Government and the law, despite the mercy of the Crown, and in the face of hundreds of a rebellious mob, who upon this occasion had law and justice entirely on their side! Thus partially does Lord Macaulay deal with the only authority he quotes for a highly criminative episode in his own history, incredible even as he has given it. But had he, instead of omitting, in his too select extract, Wodrow's lame and impotent conclusion, fulfilled his own duty as a historian, by following out the hint, and consulting the *now* very accessible records of the Privy Council, he would there have discovered a most important *additional* fact, so utterly incompatible with Wodrow's romance, as to suggest a strong motive for that disingenuous martyrologist's very convenient *abridgment* of a record which, in his day, was all but absolutely inaccessible to the public.

SECTION III.

The Reprieve of the Wigtown Women, as recorded in the Register of the Privy Council, not fully or fairly given by Wodrow in his Extract therefrom.

Distinctly engrossed in one of the best preserved books of the *Acta* of the Privy Council for the year 1685, appears the following entry, being that which Wodrow leads his readers to suppose he had quoted *verbatim*, but of which, it will be seen, he had withheld from the public both the *substantial form* and a *most important particular.*

" The Lords of his Majesty's Privy Councill doe hereby reprive the execution of the sentance of death pronounced by the Justices against *Margret Wilson* and *Margret Lauchlison* untill the   day of
            , and discharges *the Magistrates of Edinburgh* for putting of the said sentence to execution against them untill the forsaid day   And

recommends the said *Margret Wilson* and *Margret Lauchlison*, to the Lords Secretaries of State, to interpose with his most sacred Majesty for the royall remission to them "

The sederunt of Privy Council, under which this reprieve (unquestionably tantamount to a pardon) is entered, bears date the last day of April 1685. There is recorded, as being present at that sederunt, besides the other councillors, the Lord High Commissioner (Queensberry), representing his Majesty; the Lord Chancellor; the Lord President of the Session; the *Lord Advocate* (Sir George Mackenzie); the Lord Justice-Clerk; and two ordinary Lords of Session. They are entered in the register in this form and order :—

" *Apud Edinburgum, ultimo die Aprilis* 1685

" His Majesty's High Commissioner, his Grace.

Chancellor,	Tweedale,	President of Session,
Atholl,	Balcarres,	Advocate,
Drumlanrig,	Kintore,	Justice-Clerk,
Strathmore,	Viscount Tarbat,	Castlehill,
Southesque,	Livingstoun,	Sir George Monro,
Panmuir,	Kinnaird,	Gosfoord "

Until the author of these pages, who had learnt to distrust Wodrow's abridgments, examined the register for himself, and published the above in Memorials of Dundee, the very important circumstance, withheld by the martyrologist, had *never been revealed at all*, namely, that these two women, at the date of their reprieve, 30th April 1685, were lodged in the Tolbooth of *Edinburgh*, under the executive jurisdiction of the Magistrates of the metropolis, and that by this time the local authorities, whom Wodrow calls " the people at Wigtown," had *nothing whatever to do with them.*

One important document connected with the pardon of these women Wodrow seems never to have stumbled upon. Among such of the loose drafts and warrants of the Privy Council proceedings as still exist among the records of the Register House of Edinburgh, there is yet preserved the *original petition for mercy* of *Margaret Lauchlison*, the elder of these two delinquents. It is duly authenticated by a notary-public, and two witnesses, at the desire of the petitioner, who declared she could not write. Upon this petition her reprieve and consequent pardon had followed :—

' Unto his Grace my Lord High Commissioner, and remanent Lords of his Majesties most Honourable Privie Counsell

" The humble supplication of *Margaret Lachlisone* and now prisoner in the Tolbuith of Wigton

" Sheweth

" That, whereas I being justlie condemned to die, by the Lords Commissioners of his Majesties most Honourable Privie Counsell and Justiciarie, in ane Court holden at Wigtoune the threttein day of Apryle *instant*, for my *not disowning* that traiterous *Apollogetical Declaration*, laithe affixed at severall *paroch churches* within this kingdom, and my *refusing the Oath of Abjuration of the saymein*, which was occasioned by my not perusing the saymein And now, I haveing considdered the said declaratione, doe acknowledge the saymein to be traiterous, and tends to nothing but rebellione and seditione, and to be quyt contrair unto the wrytin word of God, and am content to *abjure the same with my whol heart and soull*

" May it therefon please your Grace, and remanent Lords, as said is, to take my cais to your serious consideratione, being *about the age of thre scor ten years*, and to take pitie and compassione on me, and recall the foirsaid sentance so justlie pronuncet against me ; and to *grant warrand*, to any your Grace thinks fit, to *administrat the Oath of Abjuration to me;* and, upon my takeing of it, to order my liberatione, and your supplicant shall leive heirafter ane good and faithfull subject in tyme cuming ; and shall frequent the ordinances, and live regulaily, and give what other obedience your Grace, and remanent Lords, sall prescryve thereanent ; and your Petitioner shall ever pray

"*De mandato dictæ Margaretæ Lauchlisone, scribere nec,en, ut asserunt, ego Gulielmus Moir, notarius publicus, subscribo, testante hoc meo chyrographo,*—

" J Dunbar, *witness*

" Will Goidoun, *witness* "

And now we are out of the regions of romance and martyrological rhodomontade, and can plant a firm foot upon historical record. These two women, condemned at Wigtown, had been allowed to petition the Privy Council for a remission of their sentence, upon their taking the Abjuration Oath, which they had obstinately refused before, but which they now craved should be administered to them by warrant of the Privy Council. The immediate consequence had been, that they were removed to head-quarters in Edinburgh, and that the Oath of Abjuration had been taken by them there, under the authority of the Privy Council, who had then pardoned these repentant convicts, in the form of a reprieve *sine die*, which of course had to be remitted to London for the formal sanction of the Crown.

The petition of the younger female has not been discovered.
But there can be no rational doubt that her reprieve had in
like manner proceeded upon her application for mercy, and
repentant willingness to take the Oath of Abjuration. They
had both cried *peccavi*, and so were reprieved together, indicating that they had been tried and condemned together.
And as for the child, " not thirteen years of age," who figures
so conspicuously in Wodrow's romance, as she is not included
in the reprieve with her elder sister, we may rest assured that
she had not been condemned, and had not been tried.

It seems, however, that we are not to be allowed, without a
struggle at least, the benefit of this powerful antidote, against
Wodrow's poison, derived from a fuller and more accurate
extract, of the public record in question, than he chose to furnish in his History. The great martyrologist of the Revolution has obtained, in our times, a clerical coadjutor, who, by a
bolder step than Lord Macaulay's silence, did his best still to
deprive the public of that fact, appearing as it does in the
original record of the reprieve, and which is so very germain
to the question of this martyrdom at Wigtown.

In a clap-trap volume, entitled " The Ladies of the Covenant," got up by " the Rev. James Anderson," in 1851, the
reprieve, and the old woman's petition, are both published
from the Privy Council records, and as if *verbatim*. But the
reverend gentleman had silently substituted the word " Wigtown " for " Edinburgh," although the latter is perfectly dis-
tinct in the record itself, as will be seen from the following
fac-simile :—

And discharges the Magistrates of
Edinburgh for putting of the said sentence
to operation against them

Of course this author could not afford to lose these two
" Ladies of the Covenant; " so he only quotes the petition and
reprieve, in order to enhance the *cruelty* of their execution,
which he still holds by as an unquestionable fact. " It seems,"
he concludes,—following more boldly the cue of Wodrow,—
" *highly probable* that our two martyrs were, by the *brutality*

of their judges, and the *magistrates of Wigtown*, executed *without orders* from the Government." The substitution of *Wigtown* for *Edinburgh* was certainly very essential to this "highly probable" argument.[1]

Here, however, it will be necessary to enter into some detail, in order to illustrate the nature and object of the Special Justiciary Commission, by which these two women were tried and condemned at Wigtown, but subsequently removed to Edinburgh, and pardoned there, after taking the Oath of Abjuration under the authority of the Privy Council. The nature of that absolving oath, and how it came to be high treason to refuse it (which was the crime for which these women had been subjected to a capital sentence), will be shewn in the following section.

SECTION IV.

Origin and object of Colonel James Douglas's Special Commission of Justiciary for the South and West of Scotland,— enduring from the 27th of March to the 21st of April 1685, under which the two women were condemned at Wigtown.

Towards the close of the year 1684 the armed Conventiclers of the south and west of Scotland were all astir in anxious expectation of Argyle's descent from Holland, whose invading army they were eager to join. On the 8th of November of that year the anonymous proclamation, entitled "The *Apologetical*

---

[1] Mr Anderson had still further deteriorated the value of this evidence, by omitting the fact that the old woman's petition is *formally attested by a notary public*, and not merely written by a friend. Instead of giving, or even referring to the Latin testing clause at the conclusion (a very important authentication of the document), he publishes it in this form, and under marks of quotation, as if the precise and sole authentication the petition had received :—

"Written by William Moir.
"W. Dunbar, witness.
"Will Gordoun, witness."

Declaration," first appeared in the most alarming form. It was framed in October, drawn up by the skulking but armed conventicle leader and outlaw, James Renwick, and written with his own hand, from which copy Wodrow, with marvellous effrontery, printed it in his History. It concludes in the form of a royal proclamation, thus·—"Given at   upon the 28th day of October, one thousand six hundred and eighty four years· *Let King Jesus reign, and all his enemies be scattered.*"

The Apologetical Declaration of Renwick was an outrageous repetition of the scheme of Cameron and Cargill, which had brought those " Scots Worthies " to the violent deaths they so justly met with. The renewal of it by Renwick was emboldened, to the very insanity of fanatical treason, by the murderous plots which at this time beset the Government from Holland, and the immediate prospect of Argyle's advent to seize the long coveted castle of Edinburgh for the Dutch, and eventually the Kingdom of the Covenant for himself. It was the most savage attempt to inflame the passions of the lowest classes, to incite them to murder and assassination, that ever outraged established government in a Christian country. The storm of its denunciations was directed against the highest intelligence of the land. Its *anathema maranatha* was poured out against the whole machinery, in all its departments, high and low, of law and order in a civilised state. But it shall speak for itself in the following enumeration of the objects of of its threatened vengeance :—

" Such as bloody counsellors, the members of the Justiciary Courts, generals of forces, adjutants, captains, lieutenants ; *all civil or military powers* who make it their work to embrue their hands in *our blood*, or by *obeying* such commands, such as bloody militiamen, malicious troopers, soldiers and dragoons ; likewise such *gentlemen and commons* who, through wickedness and ill-will, ride and run with the foresaid persons to lay search *for us*, or who deliver any of us into their hands, to the spilling of our blood, by enticing morally, or stirring up enemies to the taking away of our lives, such as designed and purposed, by advice, counsel, and encouragement, to proceed against us, wickedly, wittingly, and willingly ; such as *viperous and malicious Bishops and Curates*, and all such sort of intelligencers who lay out themselves to the effusion of our blood, together with all such as, in obedience to the enemies their commands, at the *sight of us* raise the hue and cry after us,—yea, and all such as *com-*

pearing before the adversaries their Courts, upon their demands, delate us, and any who befriend us, to their and our extreme hazard and suffering We say, *all and every one of such* shall be reputed by us *enemies of God,* and the *covenanted work* of Reformation, and *punished as such according to our power* and the degrees of their offence chiefly if they shall continue, *after the publication of this our Declaration,* obstinately and habitually, with malice, to proceed against us *any of the foresaid ways,* not at all *exonering from present punishment* such as *formerly* have been ringleaders, and obstinate offenders," &c

"Now, let not any think that, *our God assisting us,* we will be so *backhanded in time coming to put matters in execution* as heretofore we have been; seeing that we are bound faithfully and valiantly to maintain our Covenants and the cause of Christ," &c

Surely death, in the shape of the hangman, was grinning over Renwick's shoulder as he penned this truculent denunciation, which brought so many, and eventually himself, to the gallows. Imagine this manifesto of treason and murder levelled against the whole civilisation—the whole moral worth and intelligence, the whole conservative machinery, of the kingdom; imagine this pasted upon the church-doors and market crosses throughout the south and west of Scotland, to be read by Christian congregations entering the house of God, and the agricultural community going about their rural occupations; and then think what the Government of the Restoration had to deal with! Nor was this a mere *brutum fulmen,* to be read and laughed at or despised. Prior to the assassination of Archbishop Sharp, the same doctrines, threats, and incentives had been anonymously published, and bore ere long that execrable fruit. ' The irreligious and heterodox books called ' *Napthali* ' and ' *Jus Populi* ' (says the Lord-Advocate) had made the killing of all dissenters from Presbytery seem not only *lawful,* but even *duty,* amongst many of that profession; and, in a postscript to ' *Jus Populi,*' it was told that the sending the Archbishop of St Andrews' *head* to the king would be the *best present that could be made to Jesus Christ* "[1] Accordingly, the first manifestations of a settled purpose to murder the Primate was by a mob of "many hundreds of women" filling the Parliament Close, on the 4th of June 1674, as the Privy Council and Judges were entering the Council-Cham-

---

[1] Sir George Mackenzie's Memoirs of his Time

ber, and, on pretext of presenting a petition for "*a gospel ministry*," attacking the Primate, whom the Chancellor with some difficulty saved from these excited viragoes. "One of them," says Law, in his Memorials of the Kirk, "laid her hand upon his neck, and told him *that neck must pay for it ere all was done;* and in that guessed right." [1]

This doctrine—the lynch-law of the Kirk—became the confession of faith of the armed Conventiclers, and, indeed, was so from the dawn of Knox to the sunset of Renwick. When his proclamation appeared, followed, as forthwith it was, by practical obedience, the fate of the Primate seemed to stare every Privy-Councillor in the face. "No man," says Sir George Mackenzie in his *Vindication*, "who served the King could know whether or not his murderer was at his elbow, and they had reason to look upon *every place* as *their* scaffold, considering the violent and cruel temper of their enemies." Fountainhall, in one of his Journals of the last month of the year 1684, gives this account of Renwick's armed following: "They ridiculously keep *mock courts of justice*, and *cite* any they judge their inveterate enemies to them, and lead probation and condemn them, and afterwards *murder* them." The Lord-Register, Sir George Mackenzie of Tarbat (soon afterwards Viscount), thus reports to Queensberry, then in Dumfriesshire, by letter dated 10th November 1684 :—

"This day the Secret Committee have met on occasion of a paper affixt on the cross of Lithgow, *declaring war* with the Government, and promising to *kill us all* Since we find there is a party, declaring a war, *who lurk within us*, we think on a strict inquiry *for all in the nation* who will not *forswear* those opinions, and especially in Edinburgh, and at any rate to free the kingdom of all of them; for [hunting?] and hawking are judged absolutely insecure."

Wodrow receives no countenance for his unchristian approval of Renwick's proclamation from the Whig lawyer of the day, Fountainhall. It is highly instructive to compare his private records of it with modern Whig history on the subject.

"On the 8th of November 1684 was the Presbyterian *Declaration* (so called) affixed on sundry market-crosses and kirk-doors by the *Whigs* in

---

[1] These furies were very leniently dealt with—three of them only "were incarcerate for a time."—See *Memorials of Dundee*, vol. ii. p. 62.

the western shires, *threatening* that if the *curates* and *soldiers*[1] would not give over the persecuting and searching of them, but brought them still to public deaths, they would not spare to shed *their* blood *by their own measures,* seeing they could not do it now in a *legal judicative* way, and they disowned Charles Stuart to be their king, and in prosecution of this some of these *ruffians* fell in at Swyne Abbey, beside Blackburn in West Lothian, and *murdered* Thomas Kennoway and Duncan Stewart, two of the King's Life Guard, *in a most barbarous manner.* Some thought this *Whig* Declaration was but a *State invention,* set on foot by the *soldiers* to make that party odious and themselves necessary,[2] but this *convinced every one* of the *reality* of this declared war."

"20th November 1684.—The news came this morning to Edinburgh that some of the *desperate fanatics* had last night fallen in upon two of the King's Life Guards, viz, Thomas Kennoway, and Duncan Stewart, who were lying at Swyne Abbey, beyond Blackburn, in Linlithgowshire, and *murdered them most barbarously.* Whereupon the Privy Council ordained them to be searched for and pursued, if it were possible to apprehend them; and they called for Carmichael, landlord of the house, and examined him and others. *This was to execute what they had threatened in their declaration of war.*

Of course the King's Government became alarmed and excited. At ten in the morning of the same day the Lord Register writes to Queensberry in such agitation, that his letter can scarcely be deciphered:—"*For God's sake take care of yourself;* for now that these villains are at the utmost despair, they will act as *devils,* to whom they belong. I shall leave to write a long letter, which I intended, for now I think all other matters are to be left until those *wild cats* be catched." The great Whig Duke of the west,—who made these very "wild cats" his body-guard in Edinburgh in 1688, and, in conjunction with their denouncer, Tarbat, hounded them on the heroic Dundee,—was no less alarmed, as appears by his letter to Queensberry, dated Hamilton, 28th November 1684:—

"People hereabouts are much alarmed since the hearing of that *horrid murder* at Swyne Abbey; and they say the fugitives have been seen *more*

---

[1] It threatened, as we have seen, a great many more than the "curates and soldiers." When Fountainhall uses the term "Whigs" it will be understood that he means the *Covenanting Conventiclers*—not all the political opponents of Government.

[2] A very silly or factious idea, for which, of course, there was not a shadow of foundation. The life-guardsmen were murdered at midnight, *in their beds.*

publicly in the remote places of this shire, since the forces went out of it, than before. Wherever I heard of any, I sent and made search for the resetters, and have several prisoners. As I wrote to General Dalzell, and now to the Chancellor, without placing several garrisons in the *moorish* places of the country, it will be hard to catch or banish *these rogues*, or find out their resetters."

Five days after the date of this letter, news came to the Privy Council, that the good and brave clergyman of Carsphairn, in Galloway, had fallen another sacrifice to Renwick's proclamation. He was murdered in his own manse, at midnight, when roused from bed by a band of these ruffians. Immediately thereafter, the same gang, suddenly augmented to a hundred and eight men in arms, stormed the Tolbooth of Kirkcudbright, killed the sentinel, released the prisoners, and carried off the town drum and all the arms they could find.

The imminent danger of the crisis, both to the lieges and the monarchy, required extraordinary measures to meet it, and the utmost energy on the part of Government. For moreover, it was well known, that all this was just a somewhat premature advanced guard of the invasion from Holland, now in secret preparation, both at home and there. Patrick Walker, the chapman of treason, (himself a murderer), states, in his fanatical biography of Peden, the miraculous priest and prophet of the conventicles,—" In April 1685, Mr George Barclay and others came to the west of Scotland, in order to *engage, preach up,* and *prepare a people to join Argyle,* who came to Scotland about the middle of May thereafter, with some men, and many notable arms." Various royal commissions were rapidly issued for rooting out these invisible Thugs; and one device of a Government almost at its wits' end against this murderous revolutionary spirit, was that *Oath of Abjuration,* which the conventicle pamphleteers and modern whig historians are so fond of denouncing, and so very shy of explicitly and fairly quoting. Sir George Mackenzie himself tells us :—

"The Advocate being desired to raise processes against some who owned those pernicious principles, he prevailed with the Council to ask the opinion of *all the Judges* upon this *query,* viz., whether any of his Majesty's subjects, being questioned by his Majesty's *Judges* or *Commissioners,* if *they own* a late proclamation, *in so far as it does declare war against his sacred Majesty,* and *asserts,* that it is *lawful to kill* all those who are employed by his Majesty, are thereby guilty of *high treason,* and are *art and part* of the said treasonable declaration,—*salus Populi* requiring that *every one* should contribute what was in his power to the preservation of society?"

To this public question, a Bench composed of the most humane and learned gentlemen that ever sustained the reputation of a great judicial establishment, returned a unanimous answer in the affirmative. "It is the unanimous opinion," they replied, "of the Lords of Council and Session, that a libel in the terms of the said query, is relevant to infer the crime of treason, as *art and part* of the said treasonable Declaration, against the refusers."[1] This judicial deliverance bears date the 22d of November 1684, three days after the murder of the two life-guardsmen in their beds The *Oath of Abjuration* of 1684-5 was framed accordingly, and is as follows :—

Oath of Abjuration, 1684-5 —"I do hereby abhor, renounce, and disown, in the presence of the Almighty God, the pretended *declaration of war*, lately affixed at several parish churches, in so far as it *declares war against his sacred Majesty*, and asserts that it is *lawful to kill* such as serve his Majesty, in Church, State, army, or country, or such as act against the authors of the pretended declaration *now shown me* And I hereby utterly renounce and disown the villanous authors thereof, who did, as they call it, *statute and ordain the same*, and what is therein mentioned And I swear I shall never *assist* the authors of the said pretended declaration, or their emmissaries or adherents, in any point of punishing, *killing*, or *making of war*, any manner of way, as I shall answer to God." —(*Privy Council Register.*)

And this is that well abused *Abjuration Oath*, of the year 1684-5, which such historians as Charles Fox, and Lord Macaulay, with a very convenient *reticence* as to its real object, and actual terms, always forbear quoting, while they insinuate, or assume, that it was a jesuitical and scarcely intelligible test

---

[1] The fifteen Judges who returned this opinion were, the Earl of Perth, Chancellor ; Sir David Falconer of Newton, President ; Sir George Mackenzie of Tarbat, Lord-Register ; Sir James Foulis of Colinton, Lord-Justice-Clerk ; Sir John Lockhart, Lord Castlehill ; Sir David Balfour, Lord Forret ; Sir James Foulis, Lord Redford ; Sir Alexander Seton, Lord Pitmedden ; Sir Patrick Ogilvie, Lord Boyne ; Sir Roger Hog, Lord Harcase ; Sir Andrew Birnie, Lord Saline ; Sir George Nicholson, Lord Kenmay ; Sir Thomas Stewart, Lord Blair ; Sir Patrick Lyons, Lord Carse ; and John Wauchope, Lord Edmonstone

of *religion*, pressing severely, for dear life's sake, upon the conscience of zealots, or unfairly upon the understanding of the ignorant On the contrary, that oath was framed, after anxious judicial deliberation, expressly in reference to Renwick's Proclamation; and framed in such terms, that none but a traitor and murderer in heart and intention, if not in fact and deed, could for a moment hesitate to take it, if his mental condition were such as to qualify him to take an oath at all. The royal " Proclamation against a treasonable Declaration " of date 30th December 1684, enjoined all the lieges moving about the country to provide themselves with a legal certificate of having *abjured*, in terms of that oath, that the murderous *Thug* might not pass unseen. This stringent law, thus rendered necessary by the conduct of the conventicle leaders, was applicable to high and low, rich and poor, male and female. But, let it be borne in mind, in reference to Wodrow's calumnies, that it was expressly limited in its application to " men and women *past the age of sixteen.*"

On the 27th March 1685, a new royal Commission of Justiciary was issued by the Privy Council, for the southern and western districts, but which bore to be only in force from that date to the 20th of April thereafter, unless the term were expressly prolonged. At the head of this commission was placed the Prime Minister's brother, Colonel James Douglas of the Foot Guards. One of the special instructions under which he acted, and which had been issued at the close of the year 1684, for the direction of all the royal Commissioners, was as follows; evincing great desire on the part of the Government, even under very alarming and exciting circumstances, to act with most humane forbearance towards state criminals of the female sex ·—

" *2do.* If any person *own* the principles (of Renwick's Proclamation) or *do not disown* them, they must be *judged, at least, by three.* And you must immediately give them *a libel*, and the *names of the inquest, and witnesses*, and they, *being found guilty*, are to be hanged immediately in the place, according to law. But at this time, *you are not to examine any women*, but such as have been *active*, in the said courses, *in a signal manner*, and those are to be *drowned.*"

This was an instruction, not of barbarous cruelty, but of ·

careful criminal justice. And, as regards women, the spirit and intention was as humane as the condition of the country could possibly admit of However guilty, women were to be drowned, simply, and not *hanged as traitors*, or *dismembered*. And, in the month of May thereafter, the very month of the alleged public drowning of the women at Wigtown, an Act enforcing the application of the Test Act 1681, has this clause,—" It is always declared that this Act *extends not to women.*" Another order of Council was, that " all *women*, imprisoned for reset and converse, or *wicked principles*, are to be *liberate* on their taking the Abjuration Oath." Now this merciful disposition of the Government, towards female delinquents, a class of rebels who had been always treated, throughout both reigns of the Restoration, with a leniency out of all proportion to the murdering zeal they too frequently displayed, is totally at variance with that story of a merciless execution of two women for no other crime than " their religion." On the other hand, the *recorded fact of their pardon*, is perfectly consistent with the whole policy of the Government, and conduct of the Executive in Scotland, at the very crisis when these women were condemned. When all these circumstances come to be known, and impartially considered, the idea, that that barbarous sacrifice, the scene of which is laid at Wigtown on the 11th of May 1685, ever occurred, seems to be rendered *morally impossible.* We shall now proceed to shew that it is *physically impossible.*

SECTION V.

How the two Wigtown Women were dealt with under Colonel Douglas's Commission of Justiciary.

In terms of the royal Commission in his favour, and under these strict but humane directions from the Privy Council, Colonel James Douglas, and the Commissioners associated with him, proceeded to hold Courts between the 27th of March, and the 21st of April 1685, in the southern and western shires. Beyond the 20th of April, there was no power to act under that Commission. On the 21st of April, another royal Commission of Justiciary, for the same districts, was issued; at the head of which was placed General Drummond, Master-General of the Ordnance. This extinguished Colonel Douglas's jurisdiction, by its concluding clause.—

" And further we hereby declare all *former* Commissions granted by Us, or our Privy Council, for *trying or punishing* the said crimes in the country, either to noblemen, gentlemen, or officers of our army, to be *void and extinct* Given under our signet at Edinburgh the twenty-first day of April 1685, and of our reign the first year "

The Lord Justices for *Wigtownshire* associated with the chief commissioner Colonel Douglas, were men of high rank and position, and of different shades of politics. These were Viscount Kenmure (a notorious whig), Sir Robert Grierson of Lagg, Sir David Dunbar of Baldoon, Sir Godfrey M'Culloch of Myreton, and David Graham (the brother of Claverhouse), Sheriff-depute of Galloway. Provost Coltrane of Wigtown, who has been most virulently accused of being prominent as a merciless judge, and a cruel executioner of these alleged martyrs, was not on the Commission that tried them; and, moreover (as we shall find), was in Edinburgh, attending his Parliamentary duties there, both at the date of the trial of these women, and that of their alleged execution. The names of " Captain-Lieutenant Thomas Winram " and several other active military officers, are included in the general list (which is very voluminous) of those associated with Colonel Douglas under this Commission, who are all enjoined cordially to co-operate with him, and are placed under his orders.

While Douglas's Commission was sitting at Wigtown, two women, and *only two*, were tried and condemned to death. These were, *Margaret Lauchlison,* an old woman, stated in her petition to be " *about* the age of three-score ten years," and *Margaret Wilson,* who, in the " Cloud of Witnesses " 1714 (the *earliest* published account of the mythical romance), is called " a young woman of *scarce twenty-three* years of age," although Wodrow, Lord Macaulay, and all the modern upholders of the martyrdom, prefer, for obvious reasons, calling her "a virgin martyr of eighteen." From the manner in which their names are coupled in covenanting history, and still more from the fact that mercy was extended to both under the same deliverance of the Privy Council, there can be no doubt that they had sinned in company, and were tried and condemned together. They could not have been very conspicuous or important rebels, as their case is entirely overlooked by all the contemporaneous chroniclers, and they first emerge, as heroines and martyrs, in the fanatical *fungi* of history, engendered by the Orange regime, between twenty and thirty years after the date of their alleged sacrifice. The nature of the charge against them we only learn from the old woman's petition. She there admits having been "justly condemned to die, by the Lords Commissioners of His Majesty's most honourable Privy Council and Justiciary, in a Court held at Wigtown the 13th day of April *instant* (1685), for *not disowning that traitorous Apologetical Declaration*, lately affixed at several parish churches within this kingdom, and *refusing the Oath of Abjuration of the same*." The petition bears no date, but must have been presented between that 13th, and the following 30th of April, the date of the reprieve in Edinburgh. And this last date, be it observed, is ten days beyond the period when the Justiciary Commission, under which they were tried and sentenced at Wigtown, is declared to have become "void and extinct," either "for trying or punishing."

Had these two women submitted, at their trial, to take the Abjuration Oath, however declamatory, and publicly violent in their treason they might have been before, they would have come under that humane order of the Privy Council, by which all *women*, charged with resetting, or following, the armed conventicle rebels, or with "wicked principles" (that is, publicly proclaiming, as such women usually did, the lynch-law of the Covenant, and treasonably disowning and vilifying the Sovereign), were, nevertheless, to be "liberated," on taking the Abjuration Oath. But they must have been very obstinate at their trial; and, indeed, previously "active in such courses in a *signal* manner" (primed and goaded to their destruction by the lurking rebel field-preachers), or, according to the orders of the Privy Council, they would not have been brought under examination at all.· By the same orders, the sentence which their obstinacy, or misguided ignorance, had brought upon them, must have been sentence of death by the mitigated form of drowning. Manifestly, however, there was every desire on the part of their judges not to put that sentence into execution. The women were not ordered for immediate execution " on the place," as the instructions of the Privy Council warranted. Condemned just eight days before the expiry of that Justiciary Commission, they were allowed to petition Government. Unquestionably they were alive on the 30th of April, seventeen days after their condemnation; a fact which, in itself, is utterly subversive of the whole story of the martyrdom, namely, a *merciless* judgment, immediately followed by a *barbarous* execution. That the "*inhumanity* of *their judges* " at Wigtown, had, subsequently, effected their execution at that place, and after their special jurisdiction had expired (as some loose scribblers on the case now attempt to maintain), is manifestly nonsense on the face of it. The judges who had allowed and *furthered* their application for pardon, at a time when it was within their power and province to execute them, cannot, with any shew of reason, be imagined guilty of having lawlessly and savagely *forced on* that execution, after the appeal for mercy had been sustained at head-quarters, and the jurisdiction of those judges recalled. On the other hand, it is obvious that the judges who tried them could have done no more to save the women than what they did. The arraigned having compelled their own sentence, had become *convicts* under a decree of death, which only a higher power could reverse. To offer them the Abjuration Oath at Wigtown was *no longer within the power* of the authorities there. Condemned and sentenced under the verdict of a jury, they were out of the hands of these Lords Commissioners, and in the hands of the Privy Council. With that supreme power it now rested to say, whether the convicted were to be *allowed* to retract their defiance of the law of treason, and to have the absolving oath administered, in order that the mercy of the Crown might be extended to them.

The inevitable consequence of this state of matters was the transmission of these convicts to head-quarters, to be at the disposal of the Privy Council. But this matter is not left merely to rational conjecture. *It is distinctly indicated in their reprieve.* It is there expressly stated, that, of date 30th April 1685, the *Magistrates of Edinburgh* (and not the Magistrates of Wigtown) are, formally, discharged from putting the sentence of death into execution. The inference that they had been removed to Edinburgh is direct and inevitable. And so plainly does this fact involve the impossibility of their having been executed *at Wigtown* on the 11th of May thereafter, that the modern Wodrow school, with whom this calumnious fable of his seems to rank as holy writ, have now, for the first time, resorted to the unwarrantable assumption, against every rational view of the evidence, that the word *Edinburgh*, appearing in the record of the reprieve, must be treated as a mistake for Wigtown, committed by the Clerk of Council. That the argument in favour of this assumption is not an easy one we may judge from the fact, that the reverend author of "The Ladies of the Covenant" adopted the daring device of taking it upon himself *tacitly* to alter the public record, so as to suit that view, rather than raise the question of clerical error. Nor would we have thought it necessary to meet that theory with more than a passing remark, were it not that the Principal of a Scotch university has recently entered the arena, and boldly fathered the crude but convenient idea.

SECTION VI.

Principal Tulloch answered

Dr Tulloch, Vice-Chancellor and Senior Principal of St Andrews, Head of St Mary's College, and Primarius Professor of Divinity there, has come to the rescue of these Wigtown Martyrs; not indeed to save them from drowning, but to get them under water again. This heavy metal (enough to sink anything but these martyrs), has been brought to bear upon us in the periodical called "Macmillan's Magazine." Having no new materials of his own, however, to work with (against the unwelcome light he has received from " Memorials of Dundee ") Dr Tulloch has really done worse than nothing for the stranded saints of the Solway. Never, in common with all of his persuasion, having admitted or mooted a doubt as to this sensation martyrdom, until we had the honour of compelling his attention to the evidence, he now comes to the conclusion, as if a discovery of his own, that it is hard to say whether the women were drowned or not. Upon the whole, however, he inclines to the drowning. But even this feeble support, of the pet martyrdom of his church, is given under conditions so greatly modified, with so complete an abandonment of all the important outworks and embellishments of the story, judicial, executive, and dramatic, as entirely to exonerate the Restoration Government from having committed any such martyrdom, thus leaving Wodrow and Lord Macaulay's criminative romance in ruins, and his own theory, of a drowning nevertheless, if intelligible to himself, certainly not very intelligible to any of his readers. Yet the Principal is well satisfied with his own conclusion, which seems to be, that to shed no light upon the question at all, and to quarrel with the light that has been given him, is the most enlightened view of the subject that can be taken.

" We are *inclined*, therefore, to believe that the tradition rests upon a *basis* of fact, and that the women *really* suffered at Wigtown. This appears to us the conclusion of an *enlightened historical criticism*, in the view of all the circumstances of the case, and making every allowance for the *difficulties* it involves. Further light may be required to place this conclusion *beyond doubt*. But of one thing we feel *confident*, that arguments and *researches*, such as Mr Napier's, are not likely to settle this, or any historical difficulty His industry may be *laudable*, as his ingenuity is *fertile;* but sense, impartiality, and critical sagacity, are not only *lacking* —the writer has *no perception* of such qualities The very atmosphere of his volumes is loaded with suspicion His prejudices and *personalities* might provoke indignation, if they did not rather excite ridicule " [1]

If we have been *personal* to the kirk historian Wodrow (which is the head and front of our offending), the Principal has repaid that personality upon our own person, with all the weight that remains with the Chair of St Andrews in the nine-

[1] Conclusion of Principal Tulloch's article on the Wigtown Martyrs, in Macmillan's Magazine for December 1862.

teenth century, and some of the virulence that characterised the field-tent of the seventeenth. But we can afford to smile at this ebullition from one who, when not borrowing his narrative from Wodrow is weaving it from our pages ; and whose own ideas on the subject, but for our arguments and our researches, would never have soared beyond the martyrologist's Sprinkled throughout with such like pompous personalities, which scarcely serve to enliven an article turgid with the old unvouched accusations of cruelty that never existed, we cannot help comparing the Principal's paper to a prim old lady, described as possessing all the stiffness of the poker without any of its occasional warmth. It is not always easy to see through the "atmosphere" of Dr Tulloch's inconclusive verbiage ; but if our volumes have succeeded in destroying what really amounts to two-thirds at least of the grounds of Wodrow's martyrological *anathemas* against the Government of the latter Stuarts, surely we are justified in our *atmospheric suspicion* as to all the rest. But we accept the challenge. We pick up the professorial gauntlet, though it be somewhat soiled

Dr Tulloch, in the first place, endeavours to extricate Wodrow from the dilemma of having published the Privy Council record of the reprieve so partially as to deprive it of half its due weight with the public ; and he is also anxious to impress upon his readers that the restoration of that important proof in "Memorials of Dundee" has no merit whatever that does not belong to Wodrow, for whom he thus pleads :—

" Wodrow's quotation is substantially the same as that given by Mr Napier in his *Appendix*,[1] although the quotation is not, as it does not pretend to be, *verbatim* The only omission is, that the original document bears, that it is the *Magistrates of Edinburgh* who are discharged ' for putting of the sentence to execution ' against the women , but however important this statement may be, there is no evidence whatever that Wodrow omitted it with any design He simply *failed to see* the significance of it , or, more probably, passed it over altogether "

----

[1] In " Memorials of Dundee," vol ii. p 78 of *the text*, will be found a *verbatim* print of the recorded reprieve , and the whole question is fully argued and illustrated, from p 59 to p 99. In the Appendix (to which alone the Principal vouchsafes to refer), there is only a summary of the argument, along with a *fac-simile* of the important words which Wodrow had omitted

That Wodrow "passed it over altogether," and that, by consequence, the fact itself had remained unfruitful for a century and a half, is just the important circumstance which we claim the merit of having brought to bear upon the question of this martyrdom. But it is not so easy to be satisfied that the wily Wodrow "simply failed to see the significance of it." None so blind as those who won't see. Neither, with the original folio edition of Wodrow's History before us, can we concede, that his quotation from the Register "does not pretend to be *verbatim*." Every line of his extract is pointedly given under marks of quotation, to distinguish it from the rest of his text; and he prefaces it by saying,—" In the Council Register, since I wrote what is above, *I find what follows*." Nothing short of inspecting the Register itself, which was then in private hands,[1] and not accessible to the public, or to ordinary research, could have informed Wodrow's readers that he had not given them a complete and *verbatim* extract. Dr Tulloch's next hit is still less happy. He goes so far as to say, that this decided indication, in the Register of Privy Council, that these convicts had been removed to Edinburgh, does not amount even to "a particle of evidence" of that fact!

"Yet there is not a particle of evidence that the women were removed to Edinburgh. They were, by the evidence of the elder woman's petition, in the '*Tolbooth of Wigtown*' some time after their sentence on the 13th of April. The expression, 'Magistrates of Edinburgh,' we *cannot help thinking*, is a *clerical error*, the mark of a hasty, *concocted*, and *incomplete* document. What could have been the *use* of *dragging* the two poor women to Edinburgh, especially as, according to the theory which supposes them transported there, they had both already *abjured their crimes*, and applied for pardon."

All this is crude and confused; the hasty production of a

---

[1] In a letter addressed to the "Rev. Mr John M'Bride, minister of Belfast," dated June 21, 1715, Wodrow writes, in reference to the rise and progress of his History,—" When I went in to the Assembly, I very luckily fell upon the Registers of our Privy Council, *in the hands of a private person*, and there, indeed, I met with a *black scene*." This is a true statement of how he got at the records of the fallen dynasty, but not a true account of what he found there. If the whole of those Privy Council *Acta* and *Decreta* were published, excellent materials would be thereby afforded for a defence of the Governments of the Restoration against the calumnies of Wodrow.

mind unripe on the subject, and not at all willing to be ripened
But even the Head of a College cannot throw light upon such a
question as this without taking a little more trouble to understand it, and to be accurate and precise, instead of angry and
personal. Of course the women were in the " *Tolbooth of
Wigtown* " when their petition was preparing, immediately
after their sentence there. But how does that fact affect the
other fact, of their having been removed to Edinburgh, after
they had petitioned the Privy Council to grant warrant to have
the Abjuration Oath administered to them under an authority
which the Court that had condemned them no longer possessed? Moreover, the question was, not whether they had
" abjured *their crimes.*" They had defied the law, the King,
and the Government, by refusing to take the *Abjuration Oath*
against Renwick's treasonable proclamation, and had therefore
been condemned to death for high treason. They had *abjured
nothing* at Wigtown Nor could they, after condemnation.
But they petitioned the Privy Council *to be allowed to do so,*
though dead in law. There was every use and reason for their
being removed to Edinburgh, a very common occurrence under
the circumstances, and one which Dr Tulloch cannot deprive
of its likelihood by his verbiage of " dragging." Doubtless
the poor women went most willingly. It was following out the
object of their own petition, and assuredly was much more to
their taste than to be dragged into the water at Wigtown, in
immediate fulfilment of their sentence, as the story of this
martyrdom pretends.

And here we must take the liberty to point out, that that
loose mode of considering these convicts as having "already
abjured their crimes," has caused Dr Tulloch not to see a most
important piece of evidence, afforded by this record of the
reprieve, that cuts the whole ground from under both Wodrow
and Lord Macaulay. The martyrologist tells us, that the
" maiden of eighteen " could, by no entreaty of friends, either
during her imprisonment, trial, or execution, be brought to
take the Abjuration Oath, " but stood fast in her *integrity,* and
would not be shaken." Lord Macaulay's eloquent climax is
also entirely dependent upon that assumption in the romance :
" Will she *take the Abjuration ?* he demanded. ' Never,' she

exclaimed, ' I am Christ's, let me go,'—and the waters closed over her for the last time." Unfortunately for this flourish, the record of the reprieve affords evidence, irresistible, that both of them *had taken* the Oath of Abjuration. The old woman's petition expressly *prays to be allowed to take it*, and that they had both actually taken it, after having been condemned to death for refusing to take it, is placed beyond doubt or cavil by the terms, and by the fact, of the reprieve itself. The Lords of the Privy Council, including the Lord Advocate, " recommend the said *Margaret Wilson* and *Margaret Lauchlison* to the Lords Secretaries of State, to interpose with his most sacred Majesty for the royal remission to them." Why? Because both had *now taken* the Abjuration Oath. It could not have been otherwise. They had been condemned to die for obstinately refusing that absolving oath. Is it possible that their free pardon would have been, thus unconditionally, and in simple unqualified terms, recommended to the Crown by the Privy Council, the women still obstinately refusing to take it? Could that recommendation, made in such terms, have occurred under any other state of the case than this, that both convicts had now. contritely, come in the King's will (as, indeed, the old woman's petition expressly intimates), and *taken the oath at last?* Nor would they themselves have petitioned for mercy at all, if still in the fanatical mood of refusing to take that oath. There is no rational theory, by which other conclusion can be come to in the matter, than this, that both of these pardoned convicts had taken the Oath of Abjuration between the date of their trial, 13th April, and the date of their reprieve, the 30th of the same month. But the Principal says he cannot help *thinking*, that the word *Edinburgh*, in the record of the reprieve, is a clerical error for *Wigtown*. The wish, we suspect, is father to that thought. Doubtless there are clerical errors to be met with in the Privy Council Register, as in other old records of a like voluminous nature. We shall presently have occasion to point out a mistake of the kind; the only one, however, falling under our own observation in searching this Register. But the occurrence of any obvious, or *proved* clerical error, is no excuse whatever for *assuming* such error, where there is neither proof, nor *ex facie* indication to authorise the idea. The question here is, had these women been removed to Edinburgh, after petitioning the Privy Council to be *allowed* to retract the treasonable obstinacy under which the verdict of guilty had been pronounced against them, and to take the Abjuration Oath notwithstanding? And as removal to Edinburgh, instead of being strange and improbable, was the most likely thing to happen under the circumstances, must we *imagine* a clerical error in a fairly written public record, for no better reason than to bolster up a wild romance, most improbable in all its details, and for the truth of which not a particle of contemporaneous or legitimate evidence has ever transpired? Were it *proved*, indeed, that these two women suffered at Wigtown as narrated by Wodrow, " Edinburgh " must necessarily be assumed as a clerical error for Wigtown; because if executed there, under the jurisdiction of the Magistrates of Wigtown, they could not well be supposed to have been removed to head-quarters, so as to have come under the executive jurisdiction of the Magistrates of Edinburgh. But there being not a vestige of *proof* discovered (for contradictory fanatical tradition is anything but proof), that these women ever were executed,— on the contrary, the proof being *all the other way*,—to *think* that " Edinburgh," occurring in the Register *must* be a clerical error for Wigtown, is a thought without a shadow of reason to justify it, and not to be reconciled with that understanding of the case which can be shown to rest upon the most legitimate contemporaneous evidence, both positive and negative. Indeed so irresistible is the whole proof, that these women were not drowned at Wigtown as narrated, and so probable is their removal to Edinburgh, there to take the Oath of Abjuration, that supposing the word *Wigtown* to have been found in that record of the reprieve, the theory, that it was a clerical error for *Edinburgh*, would have been a more *legitimate* conjecture, to which the rational mind might have been driven by the nature of the proof in the case. That word, on the other hand, being found in the Register which best quadrates with all the ascertained facts, why should the Head of a College be constrained to think that it was a mistake for another word having no coherence or congruity whatever with the *proved facts* of the case? But we shall now furnish Dr Tulloch with additional materials for dissipating that somewhat misty thought.

The two Wigtown women were not the only criminals pardoned by the Government after having been condemned to death under Colonel Douglas' Justiciary Commission. He had held his Court at *Cumnock*, in the neighbouring shire of Ayr, *immediately before* sitting at Wigtown, and had there condemned *three men* to death, as appears by the following entries in the Privy Council Register :—

"9th April, 1685.—The Lord Commissioner his Grace having acquainted the Councill of ane addresse made by Allen Aitken, indweller in Cumnock, John Pearson, tailhor there, and James Meason, tailhor in Ochiltree,[1] *sentenced to die* upon the twentie day of Aprile *instant*, in a Court *held by Colonel James Douglas*, Colonel of his Majestie's Regiment of Foot Guards, for *concealing and not revealing of these rebels who lately went through some Western shires*, whereby they acknowledge their great ignorance, error, and fault, and cast themselves upon the King's mercy, and are content to *take any oaths* or obligations by law appointed, as evidence of their abhorrence of their former practices, and a testimonie of their future good behaviour, and desyreing his Grace will grant them a reprive for some time, that application might be made to his sacred Majestie for a remission to them, which addresse being read in Councill, the Lord Commissioner his Grace hath reprived, and hereby repriveth the execution of the foresaid sentence of death, untill the twentieth day of May next, at which time the same to be put in execution, in caise there be no furder order to the contraire."

Meanwhile these convicts had been removed to the *Tolbooth in Edinburgh*, to await the issue, as appears by the next entry, and had *there taken the Abjuration Oath.*

"8th May, 1685.—The Lords of his Majestie's Privy Councill, having considered the petition of James Naiper, Allan Aitken, and John Pearson, *now prisoners in the Tolbooth of the Canongate* sentenced to death by the Commissioners, appointed by the Councill, at *Cumnock*, for alleged resett, and corresponding with rebells, and thereafter, upon a former bill repryved till the twentieth of this instant, Doe hereby reprive the said James Naiper, Allan Aitken, and John Pearson, till furder ordor ;

---

[1] Here, undoubtedly, is a clerical error in the Register, which, however, is made manifest, and *corrected*, by the subsequent entries. "James *Meason, tailhor* in Ochiltree," is a blunder, for "James *Napper, mason* in Ochiltree," as it is written afterwards. The source of the error is manifest.

and ordains a letter to be writ in their favors, to the Lords Secretaries of State, recommending them to interpose with his sacred Majestie, for his royall remission to the forenamed persons, *in regard they have taken the Oath of Abjuration*, and hath purged themselves on oath as to the alledged resett or harbour of rebells, except what was accidentall."

The next entry relating to these men is dated the 5th of June, and that order, it will be observed, " discharges the Magistrates of *Edinburgh* to put the said sentence in execution," precisely as they were discharged on the 30th of April, in the case of the women sent from Wigtown.

" 5th June, 1685.—The Lords of his Majestie's Privy Councill, haveing considered ane address made to them by Allan Aitken in Cumnock, John Pearson, taillour there, and James Napper, mason in Ochiltree, *sentenced by Colonel Douglas to die*, and the Councill haveing, upon the nynth day of Aprile last, upon ane address made by the saids persons, did [*sic*] reprive the sentence of death pronounced against them, to the twentieth day of June *instant*, desyreing that the forsaid sentence might be continowed for some longer time, that application might be made to his most sacred Majestie for his royall remission, *in regard they have sworn and subscrived the oath of the test*, doe hereby reprive the execution of the said sentence untill the first Friday of December next, and in the mean tyme *discharges the Magistrates of Edinburgh* to put the said sentence in execution, but to continow the saids persons in prison untill the said day ; and ordains a letter to be writt to the Lords Secretaries of State to interpose with his sacred Majesty for his gracious remission to them, for their life only

" Follows the tenor of the letter direct to the Lords Secretaries in favors of the said three persons —

" My Lords,—

" There being ane address made to the Lords of Privy Councill, by Allan Aitken in Cumnock, John Pearson, taillour there, and James Napper, mason in Ochiltree, sentenced by Colonell Douglas to dy, for concealing and not revealing of these rebells who went through some Western shires *in armes*, whereby they acknowledge their great ignorance, error and cryme, and cast themselves upon the King's mercy, desyreing that the execution of the said sentance might be reprived for such competent time as that application may be made for them to his sacred Majesty for his gracious remission to them, for their lifes only, to be expede the several offices *gratis*. The Council have thought fitt, in regard of the penitence of the saids three persons, and that they *have sworn and subscrived the oath of the test*, to repryve the execution of the said sentance untill December next ; and in the mean tyme to recommend to your Lordships to interpose with the King's Majestie for a remission to them, for their lives only, to be passed through the severall offices *gratis*, because *of their known poverty and indigency* This in name of the Councill is signified to your Lordships by, my Lords, your Lordships' most humble servant, *sic subscribitur*, PERTH, *Cancell*. I P D "

The next order on the subject, is dated on the last day of June, from which it appears that the royal confirmation, of the pardon by the Privy Council, had arrived of that date.

" Last day of June, 1685 —His Majestie's remission to Allan Aitken, John Pearson, and James Naipper, who was accessory to the rebellion of Bothwell Bridge, being produced by the Lord High Chancellor, *Ordered* that the same be delivered to the King's Sollicitors to be by them exped the severall offices *gratis*, conform to the tenor thereof " [1]

Here, then, is further evidence of humane dispositions, and humane dealing, both on the part of the Lords Commissioners of Justiciary, and of the Privy Council. The case of the Cumnock men was of far more importance, and consequently of more dubiety as to the question of pardon, than that of the Wigtown women. Accordingly, the entries in the Register, relating to the male rebels are more frequent, and much fuller, than what appears relative to the women. In the latter case, the day appointed for their execution at Wigtown is not mentioned And no day is appointed for their *contingent* execution under the jurisdiction of the Magistrates of Edinburgh. They are reprieved *sine die*, as if their pardon was certain. Nor was it possible, under the circumstances, that their remission would be refused by the Crown. In other respects, and as regards the removal to Edinburgh, the case of the Wigtown women was just, *mutatis mutandis*, the case of the Cumnock men. These last had been escorted to Edinburgh, of some date between the 9th of April and the 8th of May. The women must have been removed on some day between the 13th and the 30th of April. Now, *between these two last dates* is just the most probable period within which the men had been removed, seeing that the *first* consideration of their petition by the Privy Council is dated the 9th of April, and they were certainly in Edinburgh before the 8th of May. Can we doubt that the whole of these petitioning convicts, men and women,

---

[1] We have not been able to discover in the Register-House any official register of the remission by the Crown, either in the case of the men or the women. But the confirmation was matter of course, especially as regards the case of the women.

were transmitted to head-quarters under the same escort? Their cases being precisely similar, as regards their position with Government, all and each of them having been condemned about the same time, in nearly the same locality, under the same Justiciary Commission, are we to believe, and in the face of the public record indicating the contrary, that the petitioning women were retained in Wigtown at the very time when the petitioning men were escorted from Cumnock? Or will Dr Tulloch still be constrained to think that the word *Edinburgh*, in like manner occurring in the reprieve of the men, is a clerical error for *Cumnock?*

But the Senior Principal of St Andrews (in whose presence we have never happened to stand), though weak in research, and weaker in argument, is strong in reproof. He twaddles over the martyrs, but he thunders upon us. *Ex cathedra*, he pronounces us to be a sort of literary *Lagg*. Drawing a severe distinction. he says we not merely *lack* sense, impartiality, and critical sagacity, but have *no perception* of such qualities. The fatherly object of the Principal is to teach us the courtesies of criticism, and the politeness of polemics So he tells us that we are only saved from provoking indignation by our exciting ridicule; and that our Memorials of Dundee are written in " a spirit which we can scarcely trust ourselves to criticise, *so absolutely is it beneath*, not to say the dignity of history, but *the courtesies of any species of literature whatever!*"

In redeeming Montrose and Dundee from Presbyterian calumnies in which courtesy never formed an ingredient, we were not writing history, but exposing falsehood. We made no attempt to dress by the purists in historical composition, being too busy detecting the calumnies of history to think of exemplifying the dignity of her march Coming into collision with the falsest and least dignified of historians, we did not seek to fashion a single phrase to that mincing, and more marketable, mode of half-complimentary dislike, which, sacrificing the expression of a just indignation to a timid rather than a fastidious taste, fears to call a spade a spade. Still we were scrupulous in obeying that golden rule of history, to be no less fearful of recording falsehood, than fearless in exposing it.

Accordingly, upon a searching investigation of Wodrow's merits as a martyrologist, after tracing, through his own correspondence and collections, the rise and progress of his History of the Sufferings of the Kirk, the spirit of its conception, the trick of its composition, and the sources of its information, we came to a conscientious conclusion, that Wodrow was " a superficial fanatic,"—and we *called him so*. Again, when we tracked him through his unmeasured and interminable calumnies against all the highest personages in the realm ; when we found him accusing the great Dundee of the most brutal crimes ; viz., that he permitted his troopers to violate matrons in presence of their husbands , that he tortured to death harmless herd boys, by screwing cords round their heads into their brains ; that he slaughtered with his own hand a pious, industrious peasant, so innocent of all offence that fiendish troopers mutinied on the spot against the murderous order of their commander ; when we found Wodrow accusing Charles, sixth Earl of Home, a nobleman of the highest character, of torturing, *ex proprio motu*, and without the indispensable authority of the Privy Council, two innocent brothers, by what the martyrologist terms " the now ordinary torture of lighted matches betwixt their fingers," because they refused to tell him whether they kept the church , when we found him chuckling over the murder of Archbishop Sharp, and then accusing that worthy and Christian Prelate of having strangled an illegitimate infant of his own, and buried it under the hearth-stone ; and when we discovered that all this could be proved to be as infamously false as if the prince of liars had whispered it into his ear, we came to the conclusion, and it was a just conclusion, that Wodrow was " foul-mouthed," that he was " a low-minded Scotch dominie " of his time, that the chief sources of his annals were " feculent,"—and *we said so* Moreover, when we came to study his voluminous *Analecta*, or " Remarkable Providences chiefly relating to Scotch ministers;" when we there found him solemnly asserting that a dead child, which had been buried, pointed out its murderer with its own raised finger ; that a dead woman, in her graveclothes, sat up in bed, and, discoursing with those who watched the body, told them of the punishment she was already enduring

in the "flames of hell," that Archbishop Sharp was discovered
by his own domestics closeted with the Devil himself, and in
earnest conversation with him, that Satan, assuming the
appearance of a sailor who was at sea, habitually slept with the
sailor's wife, but at length " *gave her a nip,* and vanished,"
from which nip she suffered so cruelly " that the *minister* of
the place, and some others, *are much concerned for her,* "
when we found his vast collection of " remarkable providences "
composed of such perilous stuff as this, we came to the conclusion, surely not unreasonable, that Wodrow was " a vulgar
glutton of coarse and canting gossip,"—and *we called him so.*
And, worse than all, forming this estimate of Wodrow upon
these grounds, we dared to sum up with the indignant question,
whether the savage and low-minded cruelties, of which the
martyrologist accuses him, " is to be believed against *such a
man* as Dundee, upon the sole and unsupported authority of
such an idiot as Wodrow ?"

Hinc illæ lacrymæ Culling from three octavo volumes
every severe expression against the martyrologist he could
light upon, isolating them entirely from the context, and
stringing these peppercorns all together, the Principal offers
this, his own angry *conglomerate,* as a fair specimen of our
well spiced *pudding,* and calls it " *delirious* abuse." Such, he
says, (with another terrible flourish of the Professorial birch),
" are the choice epithets which Mr Napier, *gentleman* and
advocate, hurls at the head of the Covenanting historian."
This sort of thunder may serve to shake the ruins of St
Andrews, but moves not us. We fear not that it will affect
our character as a *gentleman,* and we defy it to injure our
practice as an *advocate.* But our difficulty is to discover, from
this paper of his, that Dr Tulloch, with all his academic titles,
is himself very highly qualified to read us a lecture, either on
the solidities of sense, or the polish of politeness,—in logic, in
criticism, or in courtesy. There is not an epithet we have
applied to the martyrologist, that is not fully justified by the
occasion, and justified in our context. There are occasions,
moreover, (and what we had to deal with is one of them), when
to oppose the energy of truthful indignation, to the virulence
of false accusations, is at once the duty of an *advocate,* and the

part of a *gentleman*. In that latter attribute, especially, we
decline the tuition of Macmillan's clerical correspondent. And
as for "delirious abuse," we would rather be delirious in the
cause of the truth and justice of history, than dogged and dull
in opposition to it.

SECTION VII.

*The evidence derived from the Records of the Privy Council,
that the Wigtown women were pardoned in Edinburgh, and
not drowned at Wigtown, corroborated by the Record of
that Royal Burgh.*

Conclusive as we have shewn the evidence to be, against the
Wigtown martyrdom, derived from the records of the Privy
Council, we do not intend to leave it without the important
corroborations with which, as might be expected, various other
authentic sources of the truth in such matters have rewarded
a careful investigation.

No record, or minutes, of these special Justiciary Circuits,
perambulating the disturbed districts of Scotland, in 1684 and
1685, have been discovered. But it occurred to the author of
these pages to institute some inquiry about the Burgh records
of *Wigtown;* and the fortunate result, after a little research,
was the disinterment from some grave of a repository of the
tattered remains of a volume of those records, embracing the
very year of the alleged Solway tragedy. As regards that
year, 1685, however, the volume happens to be perfectly entire.
Now, in that record, *no trace of this martyrdom, nor of the
names of the martyrs,* is to be met with. There is no entry
whatever, of any sederunt of the Town Council, or the Burgh
Court, during the month of May 1685. On the 15th of April,
of that year, " John Malroy, hangman," is called before the
Council, who question him as to " what was his reason to absent
himself at this time, when there was employment for him?"
This date is the second day after that on which Margaret Wil-

son and Margaret Lauchlison were tried and condemned at Wigtown; and fourteen days prior to the date of the record of their reprieve at Edinburgh. The hangman "acknowledged he was in the wrong, and was *seduced* thereto, but now acknowledges that he is the town's servant, and promised to bide by his service, but alleges that he had no benefit or salary for his service, and craved to have some allowance for time coming, which he referred to the Town Council at ane frequent meeting *after the Provost returned from Edinburgh.*" Meanwhile, during the Provost's absence, the Council appoint their Treasurer to allow the hangman four shillings *Scots*, daily, "during his abode in prison."

As the women in question had not been tried in the Burgh Court, of course we had no expectation of finding in those books any judicial record of their *trial and sentence.* But when a Royal Burgh is charged with the execution of criminals, there are certain expenses consequent upon that disagreeable duty, which necessarily enter their books, in accounting with their Treasurer. Thus we found the whole items of the expense of executing the Marquis of Montrose, even to the price of the nails for the scaffold, detailed in the Burgh books of Edinburgh. And most assuredly had the Magistrates of Wigtown been charged with the execution of these two women, and that execution had taken place, the necessary disbursements would have entered their accounts, and been noticed in their books. Considerable expense would have attended such a drowning scene as that described by the fanatical romancers; and the fact that no single item, indicating that any expense of the kind had been incurred by the Magistrates of Wigtown, amounts to excellent *negative* evidence that no such execution occurred there. This *Burgh Record*, then, affords a *complete corroboration* of the history of these State criminals, as we trace it in the records of the Privy Council.

Not only, however, is the scene of the execution laid at Wigtown, but the Provost of the Burgh, William Coltran of Drummoral, has hitherto always been made to figure as the presiding evil genius at the virgin sacrifice. Wodrow (in utter ignorance of all the facts) asserts that the trial occurred in the month of *May* 1685 (an assertion *disproved* by the old woman's

petition), and that the execution was forthwith ordered to proceed " upon the 11th *instant.*" He says that the two women,
and the child " not thirteen," were " brought to their trial
before the Laird of Lagg, Colonel David Graham, Sheriff,
Major Windram, and *Provost Cultrain,* who gave *all the three*
an indictment for rebellion," &c. The " Cloud of Witnesses "
(1714), whose rude and confused narrative Wodrow both
copies, and materially alters, has the same story The reverend author of " Ladies of the Covenant," informs us, that
" Provost Cultrain of Wigtown was a very active instrument,"
in the death of these two martyrs. And, as we shall afterwards
find, (from Wodrow's correspondence), the *ghost* of Margaret
Lauchlison actually appeared to warn that murderous Chief
Magistrate that he was on the eve of being called to his great
account, for his cruelty to herself while in the flesh. Now, in
the face of all this rubbish, which has so long debased the
Church History of Scotland, these Burgh Records of Wigtown
prove, beyond all question, that the Provost of Wigtown, during the whole period of his alleged activity in promoting this
terrible martyrdom there, was actually at head-quarters in
Edinburgh, attending his Parliamentary duties, as Commissioner
for the Royal Burgh ! While there, doubtless he would be in
communication with the Government, on the subject of the
petition for mercy, and must have been instrumental in obtain-
ing the pardon for these women, instead of presiding at their
execution. But to this important discovery we shall have
occasion to recur, in the second part of the present investigation. Meanwhile we proceed to another corroboration, of
these public records, of a still more conclusive character.

SECTION VIII.

*The evidence of the Public Records against the truth of the
drowning drama at Wigtown, corroborated by the contemporaneous and positive testimony of the Lord Advocate Sir
George Mackenzie.*

Sir George Mackenzie of Roschaugh was Lord Advocate
during the reigns both of Charles II. and James II. His official position alone occasioned the rancorous abuse poured out
against him in the feculent annals of the Covenant. This re-
fined and highly accomplished gentleman performed the functions of his laborious, and terribly responsible office, with a
humanity, under the most trying circumstances, that was equal
to his firmness. After the death of his dear friend Dundee, in
1689, and the crowning of King William, he sought, for a time,
repose and shelter among the monks of Oxford, and devoted
himself to his beloved letters. But he did not long survive.
He died, somewhat suddenly, in his lodgings in St James'
Street, London, on the 8th of May 1691. The last act of his
life, the last exercise of his able pen, was to vindicate himself,
and the Government he had served so well, from the unscrupulous accusations of the anonymous pamphleteering Cameronians. A few months after his death, there was published
in London, in the usual small quarto form of the pamplets of
the day, " A Vindication of the Government in Scotland
during the reign of King Charles II., against misrepresenta-
tions made in several scandalous pamphlets, &c. : By Sir
George Mackenzie, late Lord Advocate there." This bears to
have been " licensed September 19, 1691," four months after
his death. In that succinct and most temperate vindication,
the following remarkable passage occurs. The italics are as
they appear in the pamphlet itself :—

" There were, indeed, two women executed, and *but two in* both these
reigns, and they were punished for most heinous crimes which no sex
should defend. Their crimes were, that they had recepted, and entertained, for many months together, *the murtherers of the Archbishop of St*

Andrews, who were likewise *condemned traitors* for having been openly in rebellion at *Bothwell Bridge*, whereupon they having been prosecuted, declined the King's authority, *as being an enemy to God, and the Devil's vicegerent.* And though a pardon was offered to them upon their repentance, they were so far from accepting it, that they owned the crimes to be duties, and our accusers should remember that these women were executed for higher crimes than the following Montrose's camp, for which *fourscore women and children* were drowned, being all in one day thrown over the bridge at *Linlithgow* by the Covenanters, and six more at *Elgin* by the same faction, all without sentence, or the least formality of law." —(*Vindication*, p 20.) [1]

The importance of this evidence cannot be exaggerated. A more conclusive extinguisher, even taken by itself, of the story of the execution of the women at Wigtown, cannot well be conceived. What does it amount to? A direct and emphatic declaration, by that high official who was public prosecutor during the reigns of Charles and James,—his dying declaration, it may be called,—that throughout the whole reign of the latter monarch, in the fourth month of whose reign the drowning of these two women, for high treason, is said to have occurred, *no female State prisoner whatever* suffered the last

[1] George Ridpath (a fanatical newsmonger in London, and Wodrow's adviser and correspondent) wrote, anonymously, that grossly indecent and scandalous tract, called an " Answer to the Scotch Presbyterian Eloquence," published in London, 1693 He there speaks (p 27) of " the knavish Prelatist who got Sir George Mackenzie to *rob* one that had given *three guineas* for a stolen copy (of the *Vindication*), under a pretence that he (Sir George) would not have it published, and yet printed it himself *after Sir George's death*." This would seem to be pointed at Dundee's accomplished friend and eulogist, Dr Monro, the persecuted Principal of Edinburgh College, who is known to be the author of a tract, entitled " An Apology for the Clergy of Scotland," &c , also published in London in 1693, and in which he replies to Ridpath --" It is a lye that Sir George Mackenzie pretended he would not publish it, though he would not allow a copy *surreptitiously procured* to come abroad *without his immediate orders and directions;* and when he saw it convenient, he recommended it to *his friend* [Dr Monro] to publish it, and it might have been printed *a good while before he died*, if the *publisher* had not been diverted by many little occurrences The original copy written by Mr Andrew Johnstone, then amanuensis to Sir George Mackenzie, is still in the publisher's hands." It was necessary to note this, as some angry scribblers in the newspapers have recently pretended that there is no evidence that the " Vindication " was written by Sir George Mackenzie

punishment of the law. For there can be no doubt as to who were the two women, the " *but two,*" whom Sir George so circumstantially records (although he does not name them), as the only sufferers, of that kind, during the whole course of the reigns of the Restoration. These were *Isobel Alison* and *Marion Harvey,* who were hanged together in the Grassmarket of Edinburgh on the 26th of January 1681, in the reign of Charles II.[1] The trial for high treason, of these violent and dangerous women, was conducted in the most moderate spirit by Sir George Mackenzie in person, who did what he could to save them from their own insane excitement, goaded to their deaths by the lurking conventicle preachers. Now the justice and necessity of that public example, in that *solitary* instance of such an example occurring during the whole period of the Restoration, is fairly and fully admitted by his Whig opponent, Fountainhall, whose record and remarks upon the case are very ample.

In the second part of this investigation we shall show how it happened that the ex-Lord Advocate came to make that explicit and emphatic declaration. Meanwhile it will be observed, that this is really tantamount to a *direct declaration,* by the highest authority, that no execution, by any form, of any State criminal whatever, of the female sex, occurred in Scotland in the reign of James II. It is very remarkable that this conclusive evidence should hitherto have escaped observation, and never have been used to shake the credit of this mythical martyrdom, until we so used it in our Memorials of Dundee. But

---

[1] The identification is placed beyond question by a comparison of Sir George Mackenzie's statement, with the indictment against these two women, and record of the proceedings against them, in the books of the High Court of Justiciary, and also with Fountainhall's account of their case. Sir George's statement will not apply to the case of the *Wigtown* women, who had nothing to do with resetting the murderers of Archbishop Sharp, and there is no case which the Advocate *could* mean, other than that of the notorious one of *Isobel Alison* and *Marion Harvey,* which he conducted in person, and could not by possibility have omitted. It was necessary to note this, as Dr Tulloch (continually pressing his want of knowledge of the subject into the service of his argument) seems inclined to throw doubt upon what can only be doubted by those who have not looked closely at it.

let us see the effect it has had upon the martyrological faith of the Head of a Presbyterian College :—

" As to the *negative* evidence of Sir George Mackenzie and Lord Fountainhall, *we cannot attach much importance to either* It was Sir George's *interest* to make the best case for the Government whose servant he had been It is *perfectly possible*, that the Wigtown martyrdom may have happened *while he never heard of it* The same remark applies to Lord Fountainhall The *martyrdom* was *provincial*, and not metropolitan, like the execution of the two women to whom he refers, and of whom Sir George Mackenzie is also *supposed* to speak It was not the *regular act of the Government* (the fact of the reprieve may be allowed *so far* in exoneration), but a high-handed outrage by its *provincial agents* Nothing is *more likely* than that such an event happening in a *remote* part of Scotland, and when the means of communication were tardy beyond our present conception, did not *directly reach* either of these authorities in Scotland "—*(Paper in Macmillan's Magazine)*

Here, surely, is some slight deficiency in what the Principal terms "perception of the quality of sense." He argues, that the Lord Advocate of the Troubles, when writing his " Vindication " in 1690, might be altogether ignorant of the notorious (if true) instance of this martyrdom at Wigtown in 1685, *because* it happened in " a *remote* part of Scotland, and when the means of communication were tardy beyond our present conception." And would that reason really account for the fact, that a " high-handed outrage by provincial agents,"—an outrage involving the murder of two pardoned females, an outrage against the humane forbearance of the Lords Commissioners of Justiciary, against the merciful decree of the whole Privy Council of Scotland, judicial and executive, against the highest prerogative of the Crown,—had never reached the ear of the first law officer of the Crown (himself one of the Privy Councillors on the sederunt that reprieved the women), even after the lapse of *five years* from the time when that unparalleled outrage is said to have been perpetrated at the royal burgh of Wigtown ? But besides the incoherence of the logic, the reason is altogether futile in itself.

In reference to communication with the Government in Edinburgh, Wigtown cannot be called " a remote part of Scotland." It was the most closely watched, and strictly commanded, of the troubled districts. It was about the centre of the rebellion in the south. It was the dangerous capital of the Dalrymples It was ever kept tightly in hand. The Government were in continual and anxious communication with it. The *Whig* Lord Kenmure was the leading Commissioner for the peace in that quarter. In that Royal Commission he was associated with, (and in politics opposed to), such prominent lairds as Sir Robert Grierson of Lagg, Sir David Dunbar of Baldoon, Sir Godfrey M'Culloch of Myreton, and David Graham the Sheriff-depute. The chief magistrate of Wigtown, William Coltran of Drummoral, was Commissioner to the Parliament for that royal burgh, and was in his place in Parliament, and in communication with the Government at the very time when this alleged "high-handed outrage" was perpetrated at Wigtown. To suppose that the news of such an outrage as this (if such were conceivable) would not have reached the Privy Council and the Provost of the outraged Burgh in the course of a very few days, and have acquired publicity, and created vast excitement over all Scotland in a few weeks, argues a total want of knowledge of the state of public affairs, and of the nature and resources of Government during the period in question. That the celerity and certainty of postal communication, and the powers of locomotion, which exist now did not exist then, we need not be told. But that, in the troubled reigns of the Restoration, there was neither celerity nor certainty of communication between the great stations of Government, however distant from each other, in matters of State importance, in exigencies of vital consequence to the peace of the country and the lives of the lieges, is an idea so *jejune* as to startle us, emanating as it does from the most ancient seat of learning in Scotland. Doubtless, old people can still amuse us with their stories of snail-like progress, and postal failures, where now railway and telegram outstrip the wind, and of dangers and distresses on rugged highways now unconscious of a rut. But nothing can be more fallacious than to argue, from such reminiscences, that all the powers and resources of rapid locomotion on land must have been nearly at a stand-still in Scotland in 1685. There was not only the ordinary post, but the "flying post" between London and Edinburgh, and that flew in five days. In Scotland, expresses were running in every direction wherever rapid communication with the Government required to be kept up. When Claverhouse, in 1679, was sent to redeem matters in the south and west, the first thing he did was to organise dragoon expresses twice a week, Monday and Thursday, between and headquarters, which were both rapid and sure, as his voluminous correspondence sufficiently proves. After the Restoration the postal system was greatly improved, and well and extensively established between Edinburgh and the south and west of Scotland. It would be easy to prove by examples that the knowledge in the metropolis of any occurrence of public importance in Galloway was, at that time, a matter of very few days. But again we say, what has the theory of slow travelling to do with the question of Sir George Mackenzie's knowledge in 1690, of a very awful public outrage occurring *anywhere* in Scotland in 1685?

In a breath, with this argument, the Principal wields another, although the two cannot well stand together. He says, delivering a broadside on the opposite tack, that the ex-Lord Advocate *did know* all about the Wigtown martyrdom, but that he had *wilfully* suppressed that instance in his " Vindication," *because* " it was Sir George's *interest* to make the best case he could for the Government whose servant he had been." At that rate, he might have made a better case still, by suppressing the Grass-market martyrdom too. This touches the question of " perception of the quality of *critical sagacity.*" Sir George Mackenzie was a high-minded and very accomplished man. He pre-eminently fulfilled that character, from which the Principal seems to say we have lapsed, "*gentleman* and *advocate.*" Moreover, he was one of the most astute statesmen of his day. Irrespective of the moral question, how would the object of his " Vindication" have been served, by a dishonest suppression of that which could not be concealed? If ever there was a case in which honesty was the best policy, it was here. The *quartett* of female martyrs would have been just as efficient for his general argument as the *duet*. Sir George had retired for ever from public life, was entirely withdrawn from the scene, and could have no motive whatever for undertaking to write any defence of the Government, except the strong consciousness of being able to place the *truth* against what he well knew to be, and indignantly calls, "many dreadful lies." And, in the very jubilee of the Orange accession, was there no one to detect, and answer, this great official of the fallen dynasty, if he had perilled that very particular statement upon so weak and dangerous a foundation as the suppression of a notorious case?

Sir George Mackenzie's " Vindication " was immediately, and *specifically* answered by a bitter Cameronian pamphleteer. There was " Printed for Edward Golding, 1692," in London, an anonymous pamphlet of thirty quarto pages, entitled " A Vindication of the Presbyterians in Scotland, from the *malicious aspersions* cast upon them in a late pamphlet written by Sir George Mackenzie, late Lord Advocate there, entitled a Vindication of the Government in Scotland during the reign of Charles II., &c , by A Lover of Truth." This reply is written in the most angry spirit. It professes to furnish a specific answer to every defensive statement in Sir George's Vindication. There is noted on the margin of each particular answer, the exact page of the loyal Vindication that is being handled. Sir George's statement in question occurs on p. 20 of his pamphlet; and the number of that page of his is printed on the margin of his opponent's pamphlet, in dealing with a matter of minor importance which it contains. But to that very conspicuous and telling statement, relating to the paucity of female executions during the reigns of the Restoration, and to the *drowning of eighty-six women and children by the Covenanters,* in 1646, " A Lover of Truth " *makes no reply whatever,* even when handling, and noting, the *very page* of Sir George's " vindication " in which it occurs. That emphatic passage he entirely eschews. But referring to another page, the Cameronian pamphleteer has this paragraph :—

" Nay, 'tis sufficiently known, that *women* were not exempted from their cruelty (persons, one would think, that could never, either by their policy or their strength, undermine the Government, and *a sex* that might have expected at least some protection from *such a Prince as King Charles II. was*), but were imprisoned, fined, and *some of them executed.*"

Why, this is exactly what Sir George himself had admitted, neither less nor more! Will Doctor Tulloch explain how this

Cameronian antagonist came to be ignorant of that grand melo-drama of drowning in the reign of James II.? Or, if he knew of it, how he came to be silent on the subject, when he was speaking of *cruelty to women*, and by way of answering Sir George Mackenzie specifically, and page by page? Would he have tacitly allowed the ex-Lord Advocate to escape upon that ingenious plea of Dr Tulloch's, that it was " not the *regular* act of the Government, but a high-handed *outrage* by its *provincial agents*"? Sir George's emphatic challenge *must* have elicited, and with telling effect, the very accusation, had it been possible to make it

Well. Both of Dr Tulloch's two conflicting theories, of the ex-Advocate's omission of the Wigtown martyrdom, being equally irrational, may we not place it upon the rational theory, that the women having been *pardoned* were *not executed?* How does the Principal deal with the *reprieve?* What does he deduce from that unquestionable fact? He shall answer for himself :—

" But what solution then do the difficulties of the case admit of? If the women were drowned at Wigtown, what is to be made of the reprieve of the Council Register in Edinburgh? *To this question we do not pretend to be able to give a satisfactory answer* The fact must stand for *what it is worth*, against the tradition, the testimony of the Penninghame Record, and the anonymous pamphlet of 1690 Wodrow's *conjecture* is probably as good as any other—that the *officials* at Wigtown, with *Major Winram at their head*, carried out the sentence, notwithstanding the reprieve. Such an *outrage* would only have been consistent with the *official brutalities* that had made the *Restoration Government* odious throughout Scotland. But the reprieve may *not have been heard of* at Wigtown Is there any evidence that it ever travelled beyond the Privy Council Office?"

This is all groping in the dark. Carried out what sentence, notwithstanding the reprieve? The women were tried and sentenced at Wigtown on the 13th of April. Colonel Douglas's Commission of Justiciary was limited to the 20th of that same month. The date of their alleged martyrdom at Wigtown is the 11th of May. Did the Lords Commissioners who condemned them appoint a day for the execution that was distant a whole month from the day of the sentence, and twenty-one days beyond the termination of the powers under that Justiciary

Commission? Impossible. The Cumnock men, who were condemned under the same Commission, were sentenced to die on
the last day of it, the 20th of April. If a sentence was by way
of being "carried out" against these women at Wigtown on
the 11th of May, there could have been no ground for pretending that it was the sentence of the Wigtown Court. What
sentence, then? The Privy Council's? But the Privy Council
had *reprieved* them *sine die* on the 30th of April And were
the theory tenable, which it is not, that the Crown had *refused*
the Government recommendation in this inconsequential, and
female case, even the flying post (by which, however, that
recommendation would not be sent), could not have brought
back an answer in time to effect their execution at Wigtown
on the 11th of May, under a new sentence

The theory, then, of the reprieve not being heard of at
Wigtown, as accounting for their having "carried out the
sentence" there, will stand no inspection. The Principal must
plead his "high-handed outrage" to the top of the bent. By
the 11th of May it *must* have been known at Wigtown, that
no sentence of death was now standing against these women,
under the Commission that had expired, and was, by *royal proclamation*, declared void and extinct, both for trying and
punishing, on the 21st of April. By the 11th of May it *must*
have been known at Wigtown, that the Privy Council had
reprieved these women on the 30th of April. Wodrow's story
is, that that reprieve was obtained in Edinburgh by *Margaret
Wilson's own father*. He says that her *relatives* were present
at the execution. The Principal's argument then must be,
that *Government* had one mind on the subject, and their
Officials another; that, without an existing sentence at
all, in the face of a known reprieve, Captain-Lieutenant
Winram, of his Majesty's Scotch Dragoons, rose in rebellion against the State whose petty officer he was, took
the King's forces with him, and mutinously acting without the orders of his own Colonel, or the Commander-
in-Chief, *murdered* these two women, in presence of remonstrating relatives, and in the face of hundreds of an outraged and excited population, because they would not take the
Abjuration Oath, which he had no authority to offer, and which

they had taken already. Captain-Lieutenant Winram would have been pitched into the Solway, his troop annihilated, and the Privy Council, Claverhouse, and the Commander-in-Chief, would have endorsed the deed.

No, says our Primarius Professor of Divinity. Winram's *outrage* " would only have been *consistent* with the *official brutalities* that had made the Restoration Government odious throughout Scotland." This touches the question of " delirious abuse," and " perception of the quality of *impartiality.*" We challenge the Principal to *prove* a single " official brutality" that would justify his violent assumption. The discovery, the unwelcome discovery, of *humane dealing,* utterly subversive of a long-cherished fanatical *fable* of " official brutality," is the occasion which Dr Tulloch seizes, not to clear his own mind from the cobwebs which Wodrow has woven there, but to blow a feebler blast upon the cracked and crazy trumpet that welcomed King William to Scotland, amid an *orage* of such " delirious abuse."

SECTION IX.

Sir George Mackenzie's Statement of the precise number of Female State Criminals executed during the Reigns of the Restoration corroborated by all the Diaries and Reports of his Whig opponent Fountainhall.

Sir John Lauder, conspicuous among the most distinguished Whig lawyers who were in active employment during the reigns of the Restoration, is best known by the name of Fountainhall, a title derived from his patrimonial estate, and by which he was elevated to the Bench soon after the Revolution. Throughout his whole career at the Bar, he stood in determined and consistent, but not virulent opposition to the Government. He was of counsel for the Earl of Argyle on his trial; and his able professional services were never withheld from the unfortunate fanatics who paid the forfeit of their lives for the most insane treason, to which they were prompted by the conventicle preachers. He took great interest in all such cases, and never failed to record, in his very voluminous *notanda,* whatever was at all remarkable of the kind. But all his observations, on such cases, tend to justify the Government he opposed. Any notable instance of the trial, demeanour, or execution, especially of a State criminal, was sure to find a place in one or other of his note-books, and often in them all. These, happily, have been published of late years, to the great confusion of Wodrow's monster history. His collection of the decisions of the Lords of Council and Session, from June 6th 1678 to July 30th 1712, were published in the last century; being a very valuable work in two volumes folio, which also contains the transactions of the Privy Council, of the High Court of Justiciary, and of the Court of Exchequer; the whole being interspersed with a variety of historical facts, and many curious anecdotes. In 1840, the Bannatyne Club printed another of his valuable repertories of political and judicial history, namely, " *Historical Observes* of memorable occurrents in Church and State, from October 1680 to April 1686, by Sir John Lauder of Fountainhall." And lastly, in 1848, under the auspices of the same literary institution, appeared " *Historical Notices* of Scotish affairs, selected from the manuscripts of Sir John Lauder of Fountainhall, Bart," in two large volumes quarto, embracing the period from June 1661 to July 1688.

Here, then, are ample materials, and of the best kind, for testing the truth of that very specific statement, relative to the execution of females, by the Lord Advocate, to whom Fountainhall was continually opposed both politically and professionally. Can that statement be refuted or contradicted out of the voluminous repertories of such events so elaborately recorded by this Whig lawyer? On the contrary, Fountainhall's diaries afford a strong and exact confirmation of Sir George Mackenzie's declaration. Fountainhall records no execution of the kind, except that of these same two women, *Isobel Alison* and *Marion Harvey,* in the reign of Charles II.; and in the reign of James II. *not one.* That single occasion (for the two women were tried and executed together), he thus very fairly narrates, entirely corroborating the Lord Advocate as to the dangerous character of the rebellion of these women :—

" 26th February 1681 —There were hanged at Edinburgh two women of ordinary rank, for their uttering *treasonable words*, and *other* principles and opinions contrary to all our Government   The one was called Janet [*Isobel*] Alison, a Perth woman, the other [Marion] Harvie, from Borrowstounness.   They were of *Cameron's* faction ; bigots, and *sworn enemies to the King and Bishops*, of the *same stamp* with Rathillet ' ' Stewart, and Potter."

Now the men here named were the most truculent of the sect, fit for nothing but the gallows.   Rathillet, indeed, was ringleader in the murder of the Primate.   Fountainhall, with all his whiggism, has more sense and candour than to record these women as saints and martyrs   Sir George Mackenzie had indicted them, *inter alia*, for having resetted and harboured, for many weeks together, the murderers of the Archbishop.   But their treasonable and violent declamation against the Sovereign, before the Privy Council and the Justiciary Court, caused the Advocate to rest the case against them on the general charge, and he waived leading any evidence as to the particular charge of harbouring the murderers of the Primate. So, of that charge the jury acquitted them, but found them guilty of high treason upon their own confession.   The whig lawyer expresses a doubt as to the law of deducing high treason from *words*, however outrageous in their treasonable character, and wherever uttered, without *overt acts*.   But more especially he doubts the Government policy of honouring any *female* delinquent with *martyrdom*.   Referring to another of his own note-books, he thus continues his note on the case of the two women :—

" We debate [elsewhere] how far *men*,—for *women* are scarce to be *honoured* with that *martyrdom*, as they call it,—are to be punished *capitally*, for their bare perverse judgments without *acting*.   Some thought the threatening to *drown them* [the women] *privately in the North Loch*, without giving them the credit of a *public* suffering, would have more effectually reclaimed them nor [than] any arguments which were used , and the bringing them to a *scaffold* but disseminates the infection   However, these women proved *very obstinate*, and for *all the pains taken*, would not once acknowledge the King to be their lawful Prince, but called him *a perjured bloody man* At the stage they told, so long as they followed and heard the *Curates*, they were *swearers, Sabbath-breakers*, and with *much aversion* read the Scriptures , but found much joy upon their spirit, since they followed the *conventicle preachers* "

This completely corroborates Sir George Mackenzie in the character he gives of these viragoes, in his Vindication ; and also as to his having done every thing in his power, even after sentence, to save them from themselves and their seducers. And what period of public commotion, and what country, can be pointed to, in which the Government of an hereditary Monarchy, recently restored against anarchy and military despotism, having to deal with, and defend itself against, the most violent revolutionary agitation, garnished with murders and assassinations committed in the name of God, would not have treated such determined and dangerous women as Isobel Alison and Marion Harvey, with much less ceremony than did Sir George Mackenzie, under the Lauderdale administration ?

But were we to believe Wodrow, and his coadjutor Crookshanks, the execution of *another female* for high treason actually *did* occur in the reign of Charles II. ; namely, that of *Christian Fyff*, in 1682. This, indeed, would afford a sufficient answer to Sir George Mackenzie's precise and emphatic declaration ; and as it also happens to be a *metropolitan* case, it would deprive the ex-Lord Advocate of the pretext of ignorance, he having conducted the case himself. Upon the 27th of March 1682, this woman was indicted for high treason, rebellion, and invading a minister of the gospel in his own church, this last being a statutory crime. Her indictment, which we find in the records of the High Court of Justiciary, thus tells the story :—

" Neverless it is of veritie, that, upon Sabbath day last, the 19th day of March instant (1682), you the said Christian Fyff, did come to the old church of Edinburgh, and there, as Mr Ramsay, minister, was coming down from the pulpit after divine service in the forenoon, you did flie upon, assault, and invade him, most furiouslie, did revile and upbraid him with many opprobrious speeches, whereby the congregation, then dissolving, was put in a great fray and confusion , and you, being called before a Committee of his Majesty's Privy Council, and examined thereanent upon the 21st day of March *instant*, you did confess that you did beat the said Mr Ramsay, and in their presence called him an *unlawful minister*, and *a devil*, and not satisfied therewith, you, not only in presence of the said Committee, but in face of Council, did most treasonably decline the King's authority, and the authority of the Council, did most treasonably revile and upbraid him, called him an unlawful King, and the Judges unlawful Judges, and murderers, for pursuing and causing execute a just sentence against Mr Donald Cargill, and Hackstone of Rathillet, for open rebellion, and murdering the Archbishop of St Andrews, declaring that since Mr Donald was executed there was not a lawful minister in Scotland, and that you think it lawful, and good service to God, to kill all the Bishops of the Kingdom, and that the killing of the Archbishop was *no murder*, and therethrough you have committed and are guilty of the crimes of treason, beating and invading of a minister, which being found by an assize you ought to be punished with forfeiture of life, land, and goods, to the terror of others to commit the like hereafter "

It must be borne in mind that the life of the Primate had nearly fallen a sacrifice to such female fanatics, at the very door of the Council Chamber, some time before the ruffians massacred him on Magus Moor. And, moreover, the Government were in possession of sworn evidence, relative to that murder (the escape of the perpetrators of which had been too successfully aided by women), which might well impress upon it, that women were neither to be despised, nor tenderly dealt with, in such cases, on the score of their sex, or their ignorance. John Millar, tenant in Magask, deponed—"That, three days before the murder, some of the assassins had a meeting at *Millar's house* in Magask, where they concerted the business; that the next night they lodged at Robert Black's house, in Baldinny, *whose wife was a great instigator of the fact;* and that, at parting, when one of them *kissed her,* she prayed that God might bless and prosper them; and added these words: ' If long Leslie ' (Mr Alexander Leslie, minister of Ceres) ' be with him, *lay him on the green also;* ' to which was answered, ' *There* is the *hand that shall do it.*' "

Now, Christian Fyff was a woman precisely of this stamp. She would have murdered the minister (a most worthy clergyman) had she been able, or would have instigated any ruffian to the deed. We find her, however, figuring in Wodrow's calendar of saints and martyrs, and her case quoted in support of his own revilings of the Government, scarcely less savage and less ignorant than hers. After giving a short epitome of the crimes charged against her, he adds—" Without *any diffi-*

culty the assize bring her in guilty, and the Lords sentence her to be hanged at the Grassmarket upon the 7th of April 1682." And thus he leaves her recorded as a Grassmarket martyr, evidently believing that she suffered accordingly. Indeed, that other great covenanting authority, Crookshanks (Wodrow's parrot), says expressly, " She was sentenced to be hanged upon the 7th of April, *which was done accordingly.*"

But the woman was *not executed !* The remarkable nature of the case (but certainly not so remarkable as would have been the drowning drama at Wigtown) caused Fountainhall to note it in his Collection of Decisions, where it stands reported thus :—

" 27th March 1682 —At Criminal Court, the woman called Christian Fyffe, who had struck Mr Alexander Ramsay, the minister of Edinburgh, was condemned to be hanged on the 7th of April next, for railing upon his Majesty, calling the King a *villain*, a *knave*, an *apostate perjured man*, who deserved to be *murdered*, &c , which she *would not retract*, though *her life was offered her if she would do it* This was a wild delusion of *Cameron's sowing*. But the Privy Council, looking on her as mad, REPRIEVED her "

In this case of Christian Fyffe, then, we have no instance contradicting Sir George Mackenzie's statement. On the contrary, against the calumnious testimony both of Wodrow and Crookshanks, that this virago was a martyr to the insatiable cruelty of the Stuart Government, we learn from that higher-minded whig, Fountainhall, that her case affords another of many examples of the *humane forbearance* of that Government, in great danger, and under extreme provocation, and more especially of its *constant disposition to be merciful to ignorant women.*

SECTION X.

Sir George Mackenzie still further, and exactly, corroborated, by the calumnious Papers of Grievances and Sufferings, penned by Conventicle Preachers, and promoted by the rebellious Presbyterians in Scotland, to induce the Prince of Orange to invade the Kingdom.

The Wigtown Martyrdom is unquestionably the grandest of all the " Sufferings of the Kirk " that Wodrow has collected, and Scotland swallowed. It is the very star of Scotch martyrology. Whig history and fanatical psalmody have fed on it ever since Wodrow wrote. Charles Fox has this magniloquent sentence on the subject, in that feeble history of his, the most innocently false, and the most elegantly useless, ever written :—" Women, obstinate in their fanaticism, lest female blood should be a stain *upon the swords of soldiers* engaged in this *honourable* employment, *were drowned.*" A new view of the subject this, and utterly unknown to the historical records of Scotland. Fox himself, in his correspondence, referring to the composition of history, says, " With respect to *facts*, it is hardly possible to be too scrupulous. It is astonishing how many facts one finds related, for which there is no authority whatever." That astonishment is anything but diminished by Fox's own fragmentary essay. Could he have *proved*, against Sir George Mackenzie's statement, that any woman whatever was drowned during the whole reigns of the Restoration? Did he know what that *drowning order* of 1684–5 meant? Could he have *proved* that novel assertion of his, that women were ordered to be drowned, at that crisis, in order to spare *soldiers* the necessity of *putting them to the sword?*

But surely at the time this great event happened, supposing it to have happened as Wodrow narrates it, the scene had been impressed upon the suffering mind of Presbyterian Scotland in lines of truth that time could neither efface nor confuse. No matter whether perpetrated by the heavy-handed vengeance of the great Executive, or the " high-handed outrage " of the little Executive, whether by *ursa major* or *ursa minor*,

it must at the time have been in the heart and in the mouth of
every true-blue Presbyterian as the most clamant instance of
those popular sufferings in Scotland, which are supposed to excuse and hallow the rebellious cry to Holland, "Come thou
and take this city." What a dull boy Wodrow must have been.
He was *six years old* in 1685 the year of the Wigton martyrdom, having been born in 1679; yet we cannot find a hint in
his voluminous record of that exciting incident,—the truth of
which, he complains, was *denied* by "our Jacobites," at the
time he is writing it,—that there then lingered upon his own
mind the faintest reminiscence of such a scene having occurred
in Scotland. And this is the more remarkable that, in 1685,
Wodrow's father, who did not die until 1707, was a rebellious
field preacher, exercising that vocation in the west of Scotland
Moreover, Wodrow's father-in-law, Patrick Warner, who also
lived into the eighteenth century, and died unhanged, was a
noted firebrand in 1685. There were not two men in Scotland
upon whose minds such an event as the drowning martyrdom
at Wigtown would have made a deeper impression than upon
these two rebellious preachers. Now, there is not a trace to
be discovered in Wodrow's History, either that a shadow of the
fact of such a martyrdom dwelt in his own memory, or that he
had ever heard a word on the subject from his father, or his
father-in-law. His leading authority is *collections* made by
Robert Rowan, minister of Penningham, in 1711, and *pretended*, but always *latent*, evidence of *that date*. But he
neither quotes a reminiscence of *his own*, in 1685, nor a word
of evidence on the subject from his father, or the father of his
wife, with whom he was in constant correspondence Suppose
that our martyrologist, in reply to the *denial* of "our Jacobites" in 1710–11, had said,—"But I was six years of age
when the event happened, I *remember* the *sensation* it created;
my father taught the truths of the gospel to the *persecuted*
west in that very year; my father-in-law did the same: they
laboured in the same dangerous vineyard out of which my
father's brother was taken and hanged; the fact of the women
drowned at Wigtown was as well known to my whole parent-
age as that the sun shone in the heavens, and I have heard
them discourse of it again and again." Would that not have

been a potent answer? Nay, would that not have been the answer, had it been the case? And could it, by any possibility, have failed to be the case had that awful public scene of a female sacrifice by drowning,—the sainted aged and the innocent young,—occurred at the burgh of Wigtown on the 11th of May 1685? We have also ransacked the immense mass of Wodrow's Collections to discover any *contemporaneous* knowledge of such an event having occurred in Scotland, but in vain. But while there was nothing in Wodrow's own memory, or derived from his parents, to assure him that the Wigtown martyrdom was true, there were papers in his own possession that might have convinced him it was false. If (according to Dr Tulloch) the Lord Advocate of the day never became cognisant of it, because Wigtown was " a remote part of Scotland ," or, alternatively, that being cognisant of it, he was " interested" to suppress the instance in his " Vindication," these desperate theories can have no application to contemporaneous collectors of such " sufferings," who were unscrupulously concocting a case of *cruelty* against the Government, in aid of the Orange invasion, and gathering their instances *from Galloway itself.*

In 1686 and 1687, the Conventicle leaders, greatly encouraged and strengthened by the weak temporising policy of King James, were agitating with all their energy for the Prince of Orange, and continually framing papers of " grievances and sufferings," rudely raked together in the most contemptible form, and without the slightest regard to truth. There is a volume of Wodrow's MS. Collections which contains several of these papers, by different hands, all of them purporting to be an "Account of Sufferings in the late times, between 1660 and 1688."

1. The first of these papers is thus indexed, in the handwriting of Wodrow himself:—" Account of the Sufferings from 1660 to 1688. *Mr D. Williamson.*" There can be no doubt that this means that notorious character, the very *Don Juan* of the Covenant, Master David Williamson, who became established as minister of the West Kirk after the Revolution. This disreputable fanatic had every motive for maligning the Government under whose bann he so often placed himself, and, accordingly, he worked most zealously for the advent of the

Prince of Orange. In the paper in question, after an elaborate exposition and defence of Presbyterian principles, he comes to the usual tirade of falsehoods against the Government, as having exercised the utmost cruelty and oppression against the people of Scotland. Though very anxious to particularise, he is put to it to find specific cases in support of his sweeping accusation, but rakes together, in the accustomed form of vague and unvouched railing, all he can gather. The drowning martyrdom at Wigtown would have been invaluable to this collector. Cruelty to *women* was the very best theme he could have dwelt upon. But this erotic apostle of the Conventicles can scarcely face that accusation at all. So soon after the event as 1687, " Dainty Davie," (for so he lives in unseemly song), *knew nothing of two women having been drowned at Wigtown* in 1685. He only knew (exactly what Sir George Mackenzie told) that two women were hanged at Edinburgh in 1681. All that he was able to gather, about the martyrdom of women, is contained in the following paragraphs :—

" Several *sick women* were haled to these courts by the rude souldiours, for *not hearing the conformists*, some whereofe died within few days after they were put in prisone. As *Agnes Livistoun* in Kipen parioch. The *ministers* were imprisoned, and some of them banished, for refusing to give in bond and caution not to preach within the kingdom. Commissions are granted to souldiours, and others, as Captain Metland and Mr Ezekiel Montgomiy, to sumond all the countrey before them, and to putt them to their oath, to answer all questions they should propose. Of some they did expiscat matter of accusatione, for which they did endyte, and put them to death ; as, whether they thought Bothwel a rebellione, the killing of the Archbishope of St Andrews, murther? *Yea, women were not spared, as witness two women executed at Edinburgh.*"

And this is all that " Dainty Davie " could report or collect, in 1687, about female martyrs! Is it credible that a cruel drowning of two women at Wigtown in 1685 could have been unknown to him? Is it possible to conceive that, had any such scene occurred, (no matter whether by order of the Government, or in consequence of a *mistake* of the Government, or of a " high-handed outrage by its provincial agents "), it would not have figured conspicuously in a list of sufferings collected for such a purpose, by such an agitator as *Master David Williamson?* On the other hand, this contemporaneous witness

E

exactly corroborates the statement of Sir George Mackenzie. For there can be no question whatever, that the solitary case to which he refers, of the execution of two women, hanged at Edinburgh, is that of *Isobel Alison* and *Marion Harvey*

2. The next paper is still more important. It is indexed by Wodrow—" Representation of the grievances of the Presbyterians in Scotland to the Prince of Orrange, 1688 ;" and commences with this address :—" To his Royall Hyghnes the Prince of Orange, the Representation of the Grievances of manie, manie, thousands in the Church and Kingdome of Scotland, caused from a prevailing factione making defectione from the *lowdiable*[1] work of Reformatione at our first coming out of Popery, the year 1560, and renewed, after thirty years' defectione, in the year 1638, untill 1660 " There follows a long and elaborate exposition of grievances in Church and State, concluding with a catalogue of particular instances of alleged oppression and cruelty, in the unvouched, stereotyped form of these fanatical libels. Every legal fine for rebellious disorder is oppressive extortion. Every punishment by the Executive for seditious dealing, or the most truculent treason, is set down as cruelty or murder. Among the rebels in Scotland there was not a single criminal. In the Government, or on the Bench, there was not one righteous or just man. Such is the type and principle of all these low collections of " Sufferings," and in the one in question that postulate is pressed to the utmost What, then, of cruelty to females,—of " the drowning of women ?" It is all contained in this short sentence :—

" *Eightly* They *executed* several simple women, for *meer words*, spoken out of their zeal, but wanting knowledge.

" It is impossible to relate all their boutcheries and cruel persecutions "

This has no application to the Wigtown martyrs, or the " drowning of women." It is still those two women executed at Edinburgh, *Isobel Alison* and *Marion Harvey*. Fountainhall, as we have seen, points to the fact that they were executed for their " treasonable words, without acting ," but he

---

[1] Curiously enough, so it is written in the MS. ; probably meaning *laudable*

fairly states the nature of the case, and justifies the Government. Manifestly the drowning martyrdom at Wigtown, which here would have told so well, was also *unknown to the framer of this petition*, the date of which is prior to the landing of the Prince of Orange in England. It is entitled on the back—" A large Representation of the Grievances of Scotland, to the Prince of Orange;" and it concludes with the following recommendation:—

" It is advised, 1. That some be sent with this address to the Prince of Orange, to be delivered first to the Earle of Crawford, and other well affected noblemen and gentlemen there with him, and by them subscribed, and delyvered to the Prince 2 That the subscriptions be written in a *by* paper, relating to this address, that the names be not *published*, if it should be printed; and who subscribes would doe it in the name of a meeting of *ministers* and others, and of *many thousands* of this land, who will adhere thereto; which is to be for a call and warrant to the Prince "

3. The next paper of the kind we have to notice, is indexed by Wodrow—" Grievances from Scotland 1661 to 1688, from *Nidsdale, Anandale,* and *Gallaway.*" This, at least, does not labour under the defect which Dr Tulloch suggests against the evidence of Sir George Mackenzie, whom he assumes to be necessarily uninformed of any " suffering " that was not *metropolitan*. This is from a *provincial* collector. This is from *Galloway* itself, the classic ground of the great drowning drama, comprehending the very date, concocted soon after that most exciting event, and having the same object in view of promoting the advent of the Prince of Orange. Among the cruelties enumerated in this paper, as relates to females, we have notices of women scourged in Dumfries, and Widow M'Birnie's tyrannical treatment by the Duke of Queensberry, but not a word about the Wigtown martyrs. Again we have, in the following passage, an allusion to the two women executed at Edinburgh, " meerly for their *opinions;*" but even by this *Galloway* collector, old Margaret Lauchlison, and dear Margaret Wilson, remain unhonoured, unwept, and unsung.—

" Many ther lives taken, *men and women, meerly for ther opinion*, who could not distinguish betwixt autority and misapplyed power "

4 and 5. Other two collections of sufferings in the same volume of Wodrow's MS., by different hands, entitled, " An

other large Account of Sufferings in the *late Tymes*," and
" Grievances *from Scotland*," both in like manner, and in *precisely similar terms*, allude to the execution of the two women
at Edinburgh for their treasonable reviling of the King, and
declining his authority, but not a word of the most exciting
and conspicuous martyrdom in Scotland (had it happened), the
drowning of the Wigtown martyrs.

6. Yet another of these contemporaneous documents must
be noticed, as it happens to refer to a martyrdom, occurring
on the very day assigned as that on which the saints of the
Solway suffered, viz., the 11th of May 1685.

This manuscript is indexed by Wodrow, "Memorandum
Concerning the Garrisons and Souldiers, 1679." But it contains
much more than that, being a memorandum also " of the murders committed in the Stewartrie of *Gallaway*, by Claverhouse, Lag, Colonel Douglas, and others ; " embracing the
dates between 1679 and 1688. The following, towards the
conclusion of the paper, all relate to the year 1685 :—

" January 23d, 1685 —Cornal Douglas, with a partie of horse, killed
6 men at the Calduns [of Galloway].
" The garisons of Earlstoune, Watterhead, and Machermoor planted,
January 1685.
" Six men killed by Lag and his partie at Lockerbie, February 19,
1685. The 21st day 5 more killed by him and his partie at Kirkconnal
" The 20th of February [1685] 2 hung up upon trees, at Irongray, by
Captain Bruce.
" The Highlanders brought to the countrie the beginning of May
[1685]
" The *elivent of May* [1685] a man shot at Newtoune [of Galloway],
by Cornall Duglass and his partie, who cam in the said tyme.
" June 11 [1685] Lag and a partie of dragoons killed uther twa men
near to the place where he killed the 5 before.
" June 18 [1685] two regiments came to Newgallaway, and therefter
went to Minigaffe. They stayed a twentie dayes, and killed a number of
nolt and *sheep*, belonging to suffering men." [1]

Must we raise the dead, to prove that these women were
not drowned? Are they who say they *were* drowned, not
bound to prove anything? Here are contemporaneous accusations of oppression and cruelty, committed in *Galloway*, pre-

---

[1] Wodrow's MS Collections, Vol. XL *Advocates' Library*

ferred against the two leading Lords Commissioners of Justiciary who tried and condemned these women at Wigtown, Colonel Douglas, and Sir Robert Grierson of Lagg,—and not a hint of their cruelty to those female martyrs! Yet these are the very men upon whom the odium of having murdered them was cast in the following century The "Cloud of Witnesses," published in 1714, gives the 11th of May 1685, as the day of their martyrdom. But here we have Colonel Douglas accused of shooting a man at the Newton of Galloway (who doubtless deserved it, if shot he was), on the 11th of May 1685, the *very day of that famous scene at Wigtown*, and not a word about those blessed martyrs! Lagg's enormities, too, in Dumfries and Galloway, both immediately before and immediately after that date, are recorded against him, but not a whisper of that grand accusation which the fanatical fables, and the truthless tombstones, of the succeeding century, expressly point against that terrible ogre. And how is Wodrow to be excused? He had found the *reprieve*. He had acquired these contemporaneous documents. He had not acquired a vestige of proof to the contrary; at least, he has not given it Could any fair and rational man have avoided coming to the conclusion, that these two women had been *pardoned*, and were *not drowned?*—a conclusion to which even his own memory must have led the martyrologist, had it suited him to search it. For, in 1685, Wodrow was six years of age.

CONCLUSION.

Upon the whole of the foregoing evidence, *positive* and *negative*, we now venture to maintain, that the following propositions are so proved as to be placed beyond the power of rational contradiction. And further, that these propositions being proved, the alleged drowning of the two women at Wigtown, in 1685, becomes both *morally* and *physically* impossible.

1 Margaret Lauchlison (or M'Lauchlan), and Margaret Wilson, were tried and condemned together for high treason on the 13th of April 1685, at Wigtown, on the eve of Argyle's invasion, by a royal Commission of Justiciary, with a jury, and under a special law which had been rendered necessary for the protection of the lieges from fanatical assassinations, and of the throne against foreign invasion ; but a law of careful criminal justice, and of *great forbearance and humanity as regards traitors of the female sex.*

2. The Lords Commissioners of Justiciary who condemned these two women at Wigtown, in terms of that law, exercised their jurisdiction as humanely as the circumstances could possibly admit of, by allowing them ample time to petition the Privy Council for mercy.

3. The Privy Council of Scotland, including the representative of the Sovereign, and all the highest functionaries of the Crown and the Executive, in like manner exercised the utmost humanity of which the case admitted, by reprieving the condemned *sine die,* and recommending them to the Crown for a free pardon, upon their submission to the sovereign authority, and after having taken the Abjuration Oath of 1685, under the authority of the Privy Council at Edinburgh.

4. On the 11th of May 1685, when these two women are alleged to have been publicly executed by drowning at Wigtown, in pursuance of their sentence, they were in prison in Edinburgh, under the executive jurisdiction of the Magistrates of the Metropolis, awaiting the confirmation of their pardon from the Crown, the Provost of Wigtown being also in Edinburgh at the same time.

5. The humanity of the Lords Commissioners who tried them, of the Privy Council, the Lord High Commissioner presiding therein, and of the Crown, having been extended to these condemned females, there was no one else in the kingdom who could have any interest, or inclination, or who would have dared, or who could have contrived, to put them to death at Wigtown, in the manner described, with a show of Government authority, and of a military force that was under the orders of the Privy Council and the Commander-in-chief

6. These two women were condemned in the reign of James

II., and *no woman whatever suffered death for high treason in Scotland during that Monarch's reign.*

We have accomplished our undertaking. That was, *first*, to detect and destroy Lord Macaulay's calumny against James II., and his Government in Scotland. as to the " drowning of women," and the alleged judicial murder of these two women at Wigtown, and, *second*, to prove a difficult negative, after the lapse of nearly two centuries—viz., that the women were not in point of fact put to death at Wigtown, as fabulously narrated by Wodrow, either under a regular judicial sentence, or by a cruel and contumacious outrage, committed against the Government and the Crown, by certain official agents of Government on the spot. We lie under no further obligation, in that undertaking, to account for the origin or endurance of the popular belief, or for the various *contradictory versions* of that wild romance of martyrdom which, when discovered to be false and calumnious, becomes simply ridiculous, if not disgusting. But the long and wide prevalence of the fable, though not difficult to account for, has weight with many and the fanatical calumny is very obstinate. We propose, therefore, in a separate part of this investigation, to examine the traditionary merits of such martyrologies in Scotland, and to trace out in what manner, and to what extent, that leading martyrdom, now proved to be false, came to be received as true.

PART SECOND.

CRITICAL EXAMINATION OF THE RISE AND PROGRESS OF THE FABULOUS ROMANCE OF THE WIGTOWN MARTYRS.

PART SECOND.

CRITICAL EXAMINATION OF THE RISE AND PROGRESS OF THE FABULOUS ROMANCE OF THE WIGTOWN MARTYRS

SECTION I.

Detection of Alexander Shields' First Falsehood on the Subject of the Drowning of Women. at the close of the 17th Century

ALEXANDER SHIELDS, the author of "A Hind Let Loose," is also the author and originator of the *general* falsehood adopted by Lord Macaulay as to the habitual "drowning of women" by the Governments of the Restoration, and of the *particular* falsehood, that Margaret Wilson and Margaret Lauchlison suffered death by drowning at Wigtown on the 11th of May 1685. The following character of this man, and his insane work, is recorded by Lord Macaulay himself, in his History of England. After giving the severest character of the Cameronian Covenanters perhaps ever penned, he thus justifies himself in a note :—" If any person is inclined to suspect that I have exaggerated the *absurdity* and *ferocity* of these men, I would advise him to read two books which will convince him that I have rather *softened* than over-charged the portrait—Shields' *Hind Let Loose,* and *Faithful Contendings displayed.*" Had the noble author added the epithet *falsehood* to absurdity and ferocity, his portrait would have been as complete as it is true.

After having been obscurely employed for a time as an amanuensis in London, this Alexander Shields, a Scotch Covenanter, joined a crew of disaffected dissenters, and very soon got into hot water. His first walk in rebellion was opposition to the Oath of Allegiance; and, upon the 11th of January 1685, he was apprehended in London with some others by the City Marshal, at a private meeting in Gutter Lane, and brought before the Lord Mayor. Discovered to be a dangerous character, he was sent down to Scotland, to be dealt with there. The advent of this important personage is thus slightly noticed by Fountainhall, who had mistaken his first name:—

" 12th March 1685 —One of his Majesty's yachts arrived at Leith with seven or eight Scots prisoners tane at a conventicle in London, whereof two of them were students of divinity, the one called Mr Patrick [Alexander] Sheills, the other called Mr John Fraser, who was afterwards delivered to Mr George Scott of Pitlochy, to be transported to New Jersey I have seen a written testimony he has left, disowning the King's Church supremacy, &c. The rest were tailors and tradesmen, *bigot in their fanaticism*."

Before the Privy Council and the High Court of Justiciary, Shields did his utmost to evade the Oath of Abjuration. Not being ambitious, however, of the crown of martyrdom for himself, he submitted to *abjure* treason and murder before the Lords of Justiciary, in terms of the oath, as thus recorded against him in the books of Court, 26th March 1685.

" Mr Alexander Shiell, who was brought down prisoner from London, being examined before the said Lords (of Justiciary), did *abhorre, renunce, and disowne, in presence of the Almighty God*, the pretendit declaration of war, in so far as it declares war against his Majesty, and asserts that it is lawful to kill such as serve his Majestie in Church, State, Army, or Countrey "

Nevertheless, immediately after this, Shields commenced a secret correspondence with John Balfour of Kinloch (the murderer of the Primate), and with other truculent rebels in Holland, affecting deep sorrow of mind for having thus abjured treason and murder, and pleading compulsion as the cause of his compliance This letter being intercepted, the writer of it is again before the Lords of Justiciary, and again in an attitude of submission, on the 6th of August 1685, as also appears from their books.

"Mr Alexander Shiell having signed the Abjuration, and having owned the King's authority, but *not upon oath*, the King's Advocate, in respect thereof declared that the Justices might continue the diet against him, and the said Master Alexander did humbly beg the Lords would continue the same, which was accordingly done, and the case was referred to the Council"

To Fountainhall we are indebted for a more detailed account of the demeanour upon the latter occasion, of this unprincipled traitor, by whom so many were excited to the doom he was ever careful to avoid.

"9th August 1685.—At Criminal Court, Mr Alexander Shiells, student of divinity, sent down from England by the King last winter, and was before the Articles of Parliament. He, after much rehtation, at last consented to sign the abjuration of these treasonable principles of rising in arms, &c ; but declined to swear it, which is conform to the 23d Act of the last Parliament in 1685, not mentioning *swearing*," &c

"Sheills would have entered a protestation that he signed it only in so far as it was *consistent with his duty*, but this was utterly rejected, and he required to do it simply Then he complained, that the only liberty of a subject being that of the *freedom of judgment and thought in controverted cases*, this should be retrenched ; yet, seeing authority required him, he was content to *declare* he owned the present King, and that it was unlawful to raise war against him, or to *assassinate* his adherers yet a man might *declare* many things he could not *swear*, and he said, though he was a Presbyterian, yet he was against the imposition and the pressing of the Covenant itself, and at last he subscribed the *Abjuration* But, in regard he had *formerly retracted* his taking the said abjuration, and said he was *forced*, it was marked now that what he had done was *voluntary* They therefore resolved only to banish him "— (*Decisions*)

But this cunning criminal, who was treated with great forbearance, contrived to defeat the ends of justice, and ere long found an opportunity of illustrating what he meant by "freedom of judgment and thought in controverted cases;" the controversy being as to the right of subjects such as himself to declare civil war against the King, and to assassinate the people to any extent they might judge to be proper. He made his escape from the Tolbooth of Edinburgh on the 22d of October 1686, disguised in female attire, aided, doubtless, by such women as he accused the Government of *habitually drowning*, although that stern measure of justice was never, in any single instance, meted out to these sisters, not of mercy, but of murder.

Having thus saved his neck, and contrived to break his bonds, Alexander Shields incontinently joined the armed outlaws who rejoiced in the name of " Society People," and in the leadership of such saints as Robert Hamilton, Cameron, Cargill, and Renwick, which last was now at their head in Scotland. He who had twice solemnly abjured, and declared his *abhorrence* of Renwick's proclamation, immediately joined that desperate criminal, who was skulking in arms against the State. Wodrow thus narrates it, under the transactions of 1686 :—

" That *excellent person*, Mr Alexander Sheills, was received by the Societies He had found means to escape out of his confinement, and made an acknowledgment to the general meeting of what he thought he had *done wrong before the Justiciary* He was extremely welcome to Mr Renwick and the more judicious people among them He was mighty useful to them, and much against some of the *lengths they ran to*, and came in heartily at the Revolution, as I doubt not Mr Renwick would have done had he been alive "

We learn from Renwick's own letters to Robert Hamilton, that he considered his reception of Shields into his army of saints and martyrs, as a matter which required elaborate explanation and apology. He says, that this backslider, after having escaped from prison, joined them on the 5th of December 1686, at a meeting they were holding in Galloway, in the wood of Earlston, for preaching ; but that he was received as a *sinning* brother, and not at once admitted to their full society, until " God should touch his heart, and bring him out from his defections unto the public work." Renwick then proceeds as follows :—

" Howbeit we thought fit to employ him sometimes to go about family exercise, not seeing any reason why this should be forborne, for thereby we might attain to more clearness anent him. And, indeed, *in a certain family*, where some neighbours (as is ordinary) were gathered into the worship, I was *greatly refreshed* with what he spake from *Rom* xii 12, especially with what he had in prayer, with a *heavy lamentation*, to this purpose ·—

" ' I cannot longer contain, but I must confess unto the Lord, before this people, I am *ashamed* to off my body a *living* sacrifice to Thee ;

yet I must do it, for I, a prisoner and a preacher, *might have been a martyr*, but I, sinfully and shamefully, *saved my life with disowning thy friends* [treason and assassination'], and owning thy enemies, and it it will be *a wonder* if ever Thou put such an honourable opportunity in my hand again ' " [1]

A "wonder" it would have been, considering the pains ever taken by himself to prevent it. But Shields did a great deal more than this to establish his character as a perfect Christian, damaged as that had been by a compulsory abjuration of the tenets of murder and treason. In this same year 1687, two years after his solemn declaration of abhorrence of the proclamation of his friend and master Renwick, he published (anonymously of course), that work of his which even Lord Macaulay has visited with severe reprehension. It may be most truly characterised as the great Institute of the Lynch-law of the Kirk, supplementing and upholding Renwick's Proclamation. And therein, assuredly, he makes ample, and safe, amends for what "he had done wrong before the Justiciary." He denounces the reigning Sovereign, and all that royal race from the time of Queen Mary, as adulterous miscreants, bastards, murderers, and parricides The murdered Primate he execrates as a villain, a *sorcerer*, a murderer, and a beast of prey. He loudly proclaims the people's right of Lynch-law, in the face of an established Executive, and, quoting John Knox as a *practical* approver of such frightful doctrines, breaks forth into this indignant climax,—" Yet now *such a fact* [as the murder of Cardinal Beaton], committed upon such *another* bloody and treacherous beast, the Cardinal Prelate of Scotland, eight years agone, is generally condemned as *horrid murder!*" Moreover, that there might be no mistake as to his own enthusiastic admiration of the deed, he thus records it :—

" That truculent traitor, James Sharp, the Arch-Prelate, &c., received the *just demerit* of his perfidy, apostacy, *sorceries*, villanies, and mur-

<hr>

[1] Letter from Renwick to Robert Hamilton in Holland, January 11, 1687. From a rare volume, printed at Edinburgh 1764, containing *sixty-one* letters from Renwick to his fanatical friends, from the years 1683 to 1689 inclusive, some of them written in 1685, after the alleged martyrdom at Wigtown *Not one of Renwick's letters contain an allusion to these women*

ders,—sharp arrows of the mighty, and coals of juniper For, upon the 3d of May 1679, several *worthy gentlemen*, with some other men of *courage*, and *zeal for the cause of God*, and the good of the country, executed *righteous* judgment upon him, in Magus Muir, near St Andrews "— (*A Hind Let Loose*)

Now, it is in this very work, put forth anonymously, and under these circumstances, by this railing Rab-shakeh of the Conventicles, that the unmitigated falsehood, of the "drowning of women," by the Government of the Restoration, is first promulgated. *No single instance of the kind having ever occurred under either of those reigns*. and no instance having ever been even alleged by the bitterest calumniators of those Governments,—Alexander Shields, in 1687, thus states it in " A Hind Let Loose:"—

" Others were daily more and more confirmed in the ways of the Lord, and so strengthened by His grace, that they choose rather to endure all torture, and embrace death in its most terrible aspect, than to give the tyrant and his complices any acknowledgment, yea, not so much as to say *God save the King*, which was offered as the price of their life, and test of their acknowledgment ; but they would not *accept deliverence on these terms*, that they might obtain a better resurrection, which so enraged the *tigrish truculency* of these persecutors, that they spared neither age, sex, nor profession, the tenderness of youth did not move them to any relenting in murdering *very boys* upon this head, nor the grey hairs of the aged ; neither were *women* spared, but some were hanged, some *drowned, tied to stakes within the sea-mark*, to be devoured gradually with the growing waves, and some of them very young, some of an old age "

This unprincipled statement was published in London in 1687. Prior to the month of April in that year, the author of it had gone to Holland, and was skulking between the nest of rebellion there, and the conspirators in the south and west of Scotland, labouring in the cause of the Prince of Orange, who profited by their services, and then discarded them with contempt. In the paragraph quoted above, a specimen of the ' many dreadful lies " which Sir George Mackenzie complains, in his " Vindication," were thus anonymously published, to further the Orange invasion, and poison the minds of the vulgar, we have the *germ* of that which after the Revolution expanded into a grand melodrama of martyrdom. *No woman had been drowned.* But there was an order of Council, that, in the event of a woman being executed, she should be *drowned*, instead of being hanged or dismembered *Therefore*, women *were* drowned, and to drown them was a *constant characteristic* of the inhumanity of the Government. Such was the convenient logic of this fanatic, who was not satisfied with falsifying in his text. To catch the vulgar eye, "A Hind Let Loose" is adorned with a frontispiece, as execrable in art as the volume is in morals There, in one compartment of the wretched engraving, is represented the *dismemberment of a female* on the scaffold,—a scene which *never occurred*. In another compartment, two women are displayed *tied back to back* against the same stake in the sea, which scene *never occurred either*. But even this lie of the graver suffices to prove, that when Alexander Shields promulgated his virulence in 1687, just two years after the pardon of the female saints of the Solway, the elaborate fable as it appears in Wodrow,—who says, "the old woman's stake was a good way in beyond the other, and she was *first dispatched*, in order to *terrify* the other to a compliance," had no existence. Shields, at this time, was neither prepared to describe any such scene, nor to name any woman who had so suffered. As it is, he stands convicted of a gross falsehood, by the positive evidence of Sir George Mackenzie, and the negative evidence of Fountainhall, and *all the public records extant*, and that detection is rendered more complete by the fact, already illustrated, that all the other collections of "grievances and sufferings," concocted in Scotland for the same purpose, and at the same time by other fanatical calumniators of the Government, afford an exact though involuntary corroboration of Sir George Mackenzie's statement as to the execution of females.

SECTION II

The first specific allegation of the Drowning of Margaret Lauchlison and Margaret Wilson, traced to another falsehood published by Alexander Shields.

Does any writer whatever, anonymous or otherwise, in the 17th century, assert specifically, that these two women, *Mar-*

garet *Lauchlison* and *Margaret Wilson*, suffered death by drowning at Wigtown in the year 1685? *Not one*, except Alexander Shields himself, and two pamphleteers of the same stamp, who, in utter ignorance themselves of any such incident having occurred, merely *copied his words*. He did not, indeed, venture to make that *specific* statement in 1687, when, most probably, the two women were known to be alive. But, in 1690, emboldened by the advent of King William, ere which time the women may have died, or become expatriated, he put forth another anonymous pamphlet, based like the rest upon an utter disregard of truth, in which that famous martyrdom makes its *first* appearance.

This obscure and inconsequential performance, entirely disregarded at the time, is entitled,— " A Short Memorial of the *Sufferings* and *Grievances*, past and present, of the Presbyterians in Scotland, particularly of those of them called by nickname Cameronians : Printed in the year 1690." Where published, or by whom, is not stated. The 22d *grievance* contained in this collection, consists of the usual violent tirade against the Governments of the Restoration for alleged cruelties perpetrated upon the people of Scotland, and winds up with this intensely false statement :—

" Thus a great number of *innocent* people have been destroyed without respect to *age or sex*, some *meer boyes* have been for this hanged ; some stouping for age ; some women also hanged, and *some drowned*, because they could not satisfy the Council, Justiciary Court, and the *souldiours*, with their *thoughts about the Government.*"

The public proclamation of the lynch-law of the Conventicles, murder and assassination, followed by practical obedience on the part of armed outlaws, gave rise, as we have seen, to the remedy (whether efficient or politic is not the question), of the *Abjuration Oath*, and its preliminary examinations. This is what is meant by Alexander Shields (himself the great promulgator of those frightful doctrines), when he speaks of the innocent, of whatever age or sex, being tyrannically probed as to " their thoughts about the Government " and then indiscriminately and mercilessly executed. It will be seen that his Memorial of Grievances and Sufferings is identical in character, and of the very same low type, as those we have already quoted, that were concocted a few years before In his collection of 1690, however, Shields has afforded a detection of himself which, although too minute and obscure to attract ordinary attention, is very germain to the matter of his truth The previous collections of the same stamp had said nothing whatever of women having been drowned, and had only very shyly referred to the solitary case of the two women hanged together in 1681. But, while repeating this accusation, in similar terms, in 1690, Shields, it will be observed, boldly *interpolates* the additional accusation of the drowning of women —"some women also hanged, and *some drowned*,"—an idea never mooted by any one of the many calumnious collectors, who had immediately preceded him in the very same walk of fanatical agitation. And, moreover, at the end of this memorial, there is inserted what Shields entitles, a " List of those who were killed in cold blood, *without trial, conviction*, or *any colour of law*, by the persons underwritten , a *short hint* of those who have been *murdered* since the year 1682, will *suffee* [suffice?] " Of this list, which assumes the usual conveniently curt form, without an attempt at verification, we venture to affirm, and say advisedly, that there is not one single *item*, that is not either absolutely false, or so devoid in its statement of the spirit of truth and justice, as to be essentially false. Having stated in his " Hind Let Loose," that Government was wont, as a *general characteristic*, to drown women, tied to stakes in the flowing tide, it behoved him to furnish, in this specific list, at least *one* example of the kind. But where to find it ? Such a thing had never occurred in Scotland. A humane order, however, had been issued by the Privy Council in 1685, that women, if condemned to death as traitors, were to suffer simply by drowning, and neither to be hanged nor mangled, as might happen to traitors of the other sex. Margaret Lauchlison and Margaret Wilson happened to afford a solitary instance of two females having been so doomed together, under Colonel Douglas's Justiciary Commission at Wigtown. Accordingly Shields, with a truthless effrontery that argues the basest nature, thus framed his example on the subject —

" *Item* The said Col or Lieu -Gen James Douglas, together with the laird of Lag, and Captain Winram, most *illegally condemned*, and *most inhumanly drowned*, at stakes within the sea-mark, two women at Wig-town, viz, *Margaret Lauchlan*, upwards of sixty years, and *Margaret Wilson*, about *twenty* years of age, the foresaid fatal year, 1685 "[1]

Fortunately this venom is so brewed as to afford its own antidote The very terms of it lead to its immediate detection. It is presented as an instance of those who were "killed in cold blood, *without trial, conviction*, or *any colour of law*." But it is absolutely proved that these two women were formally tried by a Royal Commission of Justiciary, and convicted by the verdict of a jury. He says they were 'illegally condemned." Margaret Lauchlison's own petition to the Council comes to light, and is found to bear—"I being justly condemned to die, by the Lords Commissioners of his Majesty's most honourable Privy Council and Justiciary, in a Court holden at Wigtown the 13th day of April, instant," &c He means it to be inferred, that, as the *immediate* consequence of a cruel and illegal condemnation, without a trial at all, the two women were *forthwith* " most inhumanly drowned at stakes within the sea-mark." But it is proved by the public records, that, seventeen days after their trial and condemnation in Wigtown, they were alive in Edinburgh, awaiting the formal confirmation from the Crown of their pardon by the Privy Council Their *murderers*, he says, were Colonel Douglas, Sir Robert Grierson of Lagg, and Captain William But these were all members of the Royal Commission, under which not only were the women tried, but had been allowed to petition the Privy Council for their lives ; and those Commissioners were thus manifestly accessory to their reprieve and pardon. Colonel Douglas (the head of that Commission) had, in like manner, at the very same time, been accessory to the

---

[1] This *item* will be found (by those who can endure such researches), at the foot of the *second* column, p 35, and head of the *first* column, p 36, of the pamphlet in question, three copies of which are slumbering in the Advocates' Library. We are thus particular in the reference, having failed to observe the item, though frequently consulting the pamphlet when compiling " Memorials of Dundee." This accidental omission occasioned a faulty note in that work (*Appendix*, vol iii , p 699), wherein an argument is founded upon the mistaken assumption that the alleged drowning of the Wigtown women is not included in Shield's collection of sufferings, 1690.

reprieve and pardon of the three men condemned at Cumnock, criminals much more likely to be severely dealt with than the two women at Wigtown.

But while this scandalous pamphleteer thus stands convicted of another unmitigated falsehood, by evidence that cannot be questioned, that " short hint " of his just affords additional proof, that no such scene of drowning as that of the Wigtown romance, ever occurred under any circumstances If it had, there must have been a *true* version of the tragedy of 1685, which could not fail to be notorious over all Scotland in 1690. Now, surely the real story would have been more valuable to this railer than the stupid lie he records. Why, then, did he not record the truth ? Just because there was *no true story of drowning to tell.*

That this pamphlet of 1690 was written by the author of " A Hind Let Loose," we learn from Patrick Walker, who, in his life of Peden, refers to the pamphlet by its own peculiar title, and adds that it was " written by famous Master Sheills." As appears from the preface, it had originally been framed for presentation to King William, as a help and directory to the new Government, upon the fond fanatical idea that the Orange dynasty would prove the inauguration of a triumphant Millenium of the Covenant in Scotland, established upon the political views, and Christian principles, of such men as famous Master Shields. The boldness with which this violent fanatic (and a few others with him) thrust himself forward to indoctrinate the new Government, by various written manifestoes of the kind, met with a severe rebuff from King William's General Assembly convened in October 1690 Patrick Walker (who kept a shop in the High Street as a chapman, or pedlar of such inflammatory wares), complains bitterly of " not one speaking in favour " of one of these venemous papers of Shields, which he had audaciously pressed upon that General Assembly ; and he denounces as highly unjust the *recorded* opinion of the Kirk Court (when turning it out of doors), " That it contains several *peremptory, gross mistakes,* unseasonable and impracticable proposals, *uncharitable and injurious reflections.*" Indeed so useless, and dangerous, to the now triumphant Kirk, was this agitator considered, that he was compelled to cry *peccavi* even before the General Assembly (which Wodrow most disingenuously calls, " coming in heartily at the Revolution "), and to give in " his submission and subjection," whereupon he was " admonished " by the Moderator.

No marvel then, that his " Short Memorial of Sufferings and Grievances," immediately sank into obscurity, and was treated with silent contempt by all but such congenial spirits as Patrick Walker. Doubtless Sir George Mackenzie, who died in London in the spring of 1691, had never set eyes on that rubbish. He had done enough to meet it, in his reply to " A Hind Let Loose." Two pamphleteering zealots, however, caught up from him that falsehood, of the drowning of the women but only thereby furnished additional evidence of its falsity, by being unable to repeat the story in other words than what Shields had used In the year 1691 another anonymous pamphlet appeared, entitled, " A Second Vindication of the Church of Scotland," &c. This production too, *more solito*, affords " short hints " of Presbyterian sufferings; and in a slovenly manner thus repeats Alexander Shields, as to the Wigtown tragedy. The commendable caution with which he withholds the *names* of the " murderers," as given by his more unscrupulous author, and the anxious manner in which he guards himself from being held answerable for the truth of the story, is somewhat amusing. The *caveat* occurs in his preface.

" Some gentlemen (whose names, *out of respect to them I forbear to mention*) took two women, Margaret Lauchland and Margaret Wilson, the one of 60, the other of 20 years, and caused them to be tied to a stake within the sea-mark at Wigton, and left them there till the tide overflowed them, and this was done *without any legal trial*, 1685

" The *truth* of matters of fact asserted in this treatise is *not to be taken from me*, but from those who are my informers. Few of them I pretend to *personal knowledge* of; therefore, not *my veracity* is pledged for them but that of others. If I have here asserted anything that I cannot bring creditable witnesses for, let me be blamed ; but if they have deceived, or been deceived (which I hope shall not be found), *I am not to answer for that.*" [1]

---

[1] It is mentioned in " Presbyterian Eloquence Discovered " (p 71), that this pamphlet was written by " Mr Rule, who calls himself a Doctor of Medicine, for they never pretended to have any in Divinity." Rule

So this pamphleteer, too, of the year 1691, was personally, in total ignorance of any great drowning exhibition having occurred at Wigtown in 1685. Manifestly he had never heard of such a thing. And whose " veracity " was here " pledged " for the story? His veracity, whose Paper of Grievances was contemptuously rejected by the General Assembly of King William in 1690, and stands condemned on the Records of that Assembly as containing, " several *peremptory, gross mistakes, uncharitable and injurious reflections*."

Nor is this all. In 1693, another anonymous pamphleteer (George Ridpath) took the field in a tract (more than usually disreputable, from the gross and sensual indecency, both in matter and expression, of some of its outrageous calumnies) by way of answer to " Scotch Presbyterian Eloquence Discovered." [1] Ridpath, too, has his " catalogue of the *cruel and bloody* laws made by the Scots Prelatists against the Presbyterians, with *instances* of their *numerous murders and other barbarities*," &c. One " instance " is the martyrdom of the Wigtown women, given as follows:—

" The said Colonel [James Douglas], with the Laird of Lag, and Captain Winram, did *illegally condemn* and *inhumanly drown* Margaret Lauchlan, *upward of sixty* years old, and Margaret Wilson, *about twenty*, at Wigtown, fastening them to stakes within the sea-mark, all this in 1685." (P. 24)

Here, again, we have nothing but a transcript of the words of Alexander Shields, in his " short hint " of 1690, which hint has been shown to be most viciously false.

---

was a Presbyterian hack, but rather a shy one, and inclined to bolt The author of the *tract* just mentioned, quotes the passage in which Rule declines being responsible for the facts he publishes, and adds, " What can a man believe of a book that's ushered in with such a doubting and contradictory preface? "

[1] " Scotch Presbyterian Eloquence Discovered " is coarse enough ; but this arises from the nature of the subject, and it is (for the most part) well substantiated by extraneous proof, though there may be occasional exaggerations. But the answer to it by Wodrow's friend, the London newsvender Ridpath, out-Herods Herod, and is so disgustingly impure, in its calumnies against the Episcopal clergy, as to be utterly incredible, and impossible to quote, even for the purpose of refutation.

SECTION III.

*How the falsehood of the drowning of the Women at Wigtown,
first published in 1690, came to be revived in the 18th
Century, by the Collectors of Sufferings for Wodrow's
History.*

We doubt whether any such thing ever was, as the secular
history of a martyrdom, absolutely true. But we have no
doubt whatever that such a thing never was, and never will
be, as a *truthful Martyrological History*. As regards Scotland,
it is impossible. Law led by romance, or a legal judgment inspired by irregular flashes of prurient sentiment derived from a
feminine source, and expounded on erotic principles, would be
an incongruity of Jurisprudence not more to be distrusted,
than a criminative History, framed out of the passions of tur-
bulent times, by the disciples of a fanatical democracy which
had been crushed by the heavier hand of the Executive it
defied.

Contemptible as was the clique presided over, in 1690, by
the author of " A Hind Let Loose," and which the General
Assembly of the Kirk, in that year, extinguished for ever,
without an effort and without a blush, it was the true exponent of the politics and the polemics to which that now really
Venerable Assembly owes its original elevation, indeed, its
very existence, and also its present pollarded condition. In
1690 Alexander Shields was the consistent exponent of the
principles of John Knox in the murder of Cardinal Beaton
the exponent of the regime of Argyle in the murder of Montrose : the exponent of the last great success of that same
regime in the murder of Archbishop Sharp : the exponent of
the system of Cameron, Cargill, and Renwick, with whom intolerant anarchy was Christian government, and brutal assassination eternal justice. Upon this very ladder it was that the
Prince of Orange ascended to the throne of Scotland, and
then kicked from under him the rotten and gory structure.
So, Alexander Shields and his disciples (the last joint of the

rump of the old Argyle regime), reduced to the lowest ebb of agitation, betook themselves to the old resource of virulent pamphleteering, in which truth never formed an ingredient. To the ripening liberties of the country, ripening under the dispensations of Providence evolving good out of evil, in spite of, but never by means of, the Scotch Covenant, the expiring struggles of that regime did little harm. But it engendered an *incubus* upon the History of Scotland, and a gross libel upon the character of the nation,—" Wodrow's History of the Sufferings of the Church." Shaken off by the Orange Government in Scotland, like a too familiar *pediculus* crawling upon the new royal Presbyterian robe, Alexander Shields migrated to the West Indies, where he died in 1700. The reverend Robert Wodrow was worthy to succeed him as the chronicler of Kirk " Sufferings and Grievances."

Wodrow's voluminous correspondence with his fanatical friends early in the eighteenth century is full of groans at the strong national predilection for Episcopalian Church government then manifesting itself throughout Scotland, and at the sinful toleration thereof by the Orange Government. This old leaven of the tyrannical spirit of the Covenant, with which Shields had failed to inoculate King William, found a vent in raking "Sufferings and Grievances" out of the choked and ruined conduits of the Covenant, and inflating the bitter anonymous pamphlets of the "rabblers" of the Episcopal clergy into a *monstrum horrendum ingens* of that peculiar stamp of Church history. The star of Wodrow burst upon the world in the shape of two lumbering folios, the first volume appearing in 1721, and the second in 1722. For a long time this gigantic and clamorous libel was unhonoured in the republic of letters, indeed, of no account whatever, save with a sect who were willing to believe that the dead made a sign, or a cow spoke, if Wodrow said so. It was disregarded in England until Fox's posthumous fragment, professing to be a history of the early part of the reign of James II., was published in 1808. Sir Walter Scott, in 1818, speaks of " the historian Wodrow, whom Mr Fox introduced to the knowledge of the English, raising the price of his two ponderous volumes from ten shillings to two or three guineas" But.

verily, there never was a certificate of character less valuable than Fox's *imprimatur for the nonce* on Wodrow's History. Let us trace its history, which may be said to involve the history of the romance of the Wigtown martyrdom. The first ominous note of it is sounded in a letter from Wodrow to one " Mr John Cross, merchant in Glasgow," dated March 13, 1711 : —

" The *task*[1] you prescribe me is what I reckon very seasonable at this juncture, and what within a little time I hope to be in a *better case for* than I am at present, if *some collections*[2] that are at present making were put in my hands   But in this matter, of an exact collection of the sufferings of the Presbyterians, especially in the five western shires, that were to be made a hunting field in the late reign, we are too late by twenty years [3] Yet I am persuaded there may, and I hope will be, as much ⎰ gathered[4] ⎱ as may put the *Prelatists* to blush when they speak ⎱ recovered ⎰ of their persecutors,[5] and discover to the world that the barbarities in Scotland from the 1660-88, have no parallel except those exercised in France, by a friend of these persons that make such a *pother* anent *Presbyterian* persecution ; and if I be not much mistaken, there will be many *singularities* found in the *Prelatic* persecution that exceed even that of France "

Nevertheless, two years and a half after the date of this letter, we find Wodrow still groping for his " singularities "

---

[1] Dr M'Crie (the biographer of Knox), who edited (for the Wodrow Society) this among many other letters of Wodrow preserved in the Advocates' Library, prints the word *task* " talk " It is distinctly *task* in the original. The learned Doctor, as we shall find, had altogether overlooked the point of this letter

[2] Collections of " Sufferings in the late times," about which the parish ministers again busied themselves in 1710–11, in their different districts, and which scheme produced the suffering of the two Wigtown martyrs Of this afterwards.

[3] But the collectors, who commenced their task immediately after the date of the Wigtown martyrdom, and yet *omitted* that " suffering," appear to have been *too soon for the purpose.*

[4] This various reading of the important idea is written in that double form in Wodrow's own draft or transcript of the letter.

[5] This refers to the brutal " rabbling " of all the respectable clergy in the disturbed districts of Scotland, by the conventicle-excited Presbyterian mob, when military protection was suddenly withdrawn from Scotland, and the country left to the mercy of fanatics and false statesmen, at the commencement of the Revolution

that were to cause the Prelatists to blush, and seemingly still unfurnished with that grandest of all his singularities, the melo-drama of martyrdom at Wigtown In a letter to one Mr Robert Wylie, dated September 26, 1713, he writes as follows :—

"Nothing has come to me (or to the Principal [*Carstares*] before his going to Court) *anent the Sufferings* If any thing be come to your hand, I'll be glad to know I wish you would entertain thoughts of giving *some beginning* to some account of this nature For me, I can fall on *no shape*, and have *not so much as a thread of these times in my head*"

Upon this remarkable passage Dr M'Crie notes as follows·— "This is the first time that we find any *decided allusion* made by Wodrow to the project of writing a History of the Sufferings of the Church of Scotland, and it is curious to observe how little idea he then had of the vast undertaking which he was afterwards to accomplish." Curious enough. Being quite untrammelled, however, by scrupulosity as to facts, that obstacle was soon overcome. But the learned biographer of Knox had here committed a slip in his editorial functions. Wodrow's allusion to that project is just as decided in his letter to Mr John Cross, dated two years and a half earlier. It is indeed curious to find him, after that lapse of time, still confessing that he could fall on no shape, and had not a thread of those times in his memory or his mind. It is no less curious to observe how rapidly he went ahead in his "vast undertaking," when once the gathering ball was set a-rolling. On the 11th of January 1714, he thus writes to " Lt.-Colonel Erskine."

"I have this night scribbled out a very rude and imperfect sketch of *our Sufferings*, the length of *Pentland*, from what papers and materials I could have access to I find it *swell on my hand*, far beyond the first design of a *short pamphlet to spread among the country people*," &c "I think there are materials, in my *confused collection*, that may be of use to any person of qualifications suited to this task, which I am very sensible I want, and if such a person can be prevailed with to undertake it, I shall very readily communicate what I have.   Indeed, the more I dip into the *scandalous methods* of that time, the more I lament our want of a History of the *unparalleled practices* under the reigns of the two brothers, with relation to this poor Church. I resolve, if the Lord will, to go on in my *rude collections* such as they are, and, as I threated in my last, I send you this."

Saintly sufferings of this sort, thus wished for and thus fished for, very soon "swell on the hand," and "threads of these times" quickly festooned the brains of our brave martyrologist On the 26th of August 1714, he thus writes to one Mr James Hart :—

"I have *completed* my first book of the History of the Sufferings in the late times, from the *Restoration*, to *Pentland*, and drawn the first draught of the second, from *Pentland*, to *Bothwell Bridge*, which is like I may either send or bring in to you and friends at Edinburgh I reckon this great turn of affairs[1] renders this account very necessary and seasonable, though I am a very unfit hand to essay it If any thing I could collect may be materials to another in case to go through with that necessary design, I shall reckon my little pains well bestowed "

But Wodrow had as little intention of giving up the task for which he was so peculiarly well fitted, as any one else had of taking it out of his hands. On the 11th of October 1714, he thus writes to " Mr William Forbes, Professor of Law at Glasgow :—

" I send you the first draught of the first six years of our Sufferings," &c. " I could heartily wish you took Sir George Mackenzie's remarks, on the Government of King Charles the Second, in task I have an answer to it, published in London, but it's lame."[2]

In the following month, November 25, he thus unbosoms himself to " the Rev. Mr John Anderson, minister at Dumbarton," another cook to whom he had sent a portion of his *magnum opus* for revisal :—

" By your kind pains to correct and amend it, you truly encouraged me more to go on than any thing I yet met with since I entered upon it Your good wishes to so necessary a work have made you pass by far a too favourable judgment on this first book in your letter. I own the further I go on, I see the more necessity for somewhat on this head ; and if any thing I can cast together upon this head, may be of use when corrected by you and others, I shall not reckon my pains altogether lost, and nothing but a conviction of our negligence since the Revolution, and the ill consequences of it, made me, last winter, venture to give a kind of beginning to it, *almost in a fret* My hand is ill ; my style and *syllabication* have given you a great deal of trouble ; *my head is worst of all*, and I have *few or no materials* sent me However, I'll endeavour to go through with it as I can, if the Lord spare me," &c.

---

[1] Death of Queen Anne, and Accession of George I.

[2] Sir George Mackenzie's " Vindication," and the Answer to it, mentioned before.

Another letter is to that redoubtable character, King William's Scotch *factotum*, Carstares, who of course would lend his aid *con amore* to such a scheme as libelling the Government under which he himself had so justly suffered, but to which suffering he owed his life, his fame, and his fortune. On the 14th of June 1715, Wodrow thus writes to him :—

"The more I *dip* into that *dreadful time*, the greater the necessity I see of a *well touched* account of it I am truly sorry I should have been put upon the giving a beginning to a design of this nature, who was not born when many of these cruelties was acted, and have *no thread to lead me* to any enquiries into them,[1] and wish heartily it had been engaged in by any other. But since I am entered on it, and cannot say I want matter could I shape it right, I am going as far as my materials will carry me, and shall lay my rude draught before you and others, and be entirely directed what to do"

In his first letter on the subject, in 1711 (that overlooked by Dr M'Crie), it will be observed that Wodrow expresses a desire, while admitting the blank condition of his own mind as regards his project, that "some collections that are *at present making* were put in my hands." This allusion is explained in another letter of his, addressed to the Rev. John M'Bride, minister at Belfast, and dated June 21, 1715, wherein he affords this curious information :—

"Before you left this country, we were, in our *Synods and Assemblies*, talking of *collections* for a History of the Sufferings of this Church under Prelacy. *I was pitched upon to receive them*, and a very few accounts came to my hands, and I had some things, relative to that head, among the papers I had gathered together *for my own diversion*[2] It was thought necessary a beginning should be given to an account of our sufferings, and some papers being in my hand, and others promised me, I was, through my own easiness, and the importunity of others, last year (1714) put upon drawing a first draught of this work, in itself so necessary, and so much wanted. None can regret this business falling into my hands more than I do myself But, as it's usual in things of this nature, every body was willing to roll the labour and toil of it off themselves, and my excess of good nature, which brought me through importunity to essay a

---

[1] Wodrow was born in 1679, and, as already noticed, his father and his father-in-law were conventicle leaders

[2] Some of those collections of "grievances and sufferings," doubtless, between 1660 and 1688, written to promote the advent of the Prince of Orange, and which *are all silent* on the subject of the drowning of the women at Wigtown, as we have shown.

beginning to it, has now engaged me, and I must, *some way or other*, wrestle through the first rude draught of it. When I went into the Assembly, I very luckily fell upon the *Registers of our Privy Council*, in the hands of *private persons*, and there indeed I met with a *black scene*. The looking over of these kept me some while in Edinburgh, after the Assembly was up. And I am promised access to the books of our Justiciary. Materials are now swelling pretty much on my hand, and I am like to have work enough to put them in any kind of order. I have now brought my accounts down to the beginning of the 1685,[1] from the Restoration, where I begin "

Thus was Wodrow's History conceived, and born, and nourished. It was not, as Dr M'Crie was pleased to consider it, a vast historical undertaking. It was a mean conspiracy, of a fanatical sect, against the truth, justice, and common sense of History. It was that same historical undertaking, which, for a century and a half, imposed upon History, as an incontrovertible fact, the intense falsehood (among many others), that Colonel Graham of Claverhouse, the most aristocratic gentleman, the most chivalrous captain, the most clear-minded statesman of his time, did, with his own hand and pistol, and in presence of the royal troops he was commanding, blow out the brains of a pious, industrious, and inoffensive peasant, and that because his own regiment (devoted to himself) had *mutinied* on the spot against what even they considered a savage and murderous order. To " dip into that dreadful time," meant with Wodrow a species of *dipping* which may be not inaptly illustrated by reference to a pamphlet published not a hundred years ago, and entitled, ' Great Demonstration at Sanquhar, on twenty-second July 1860, in commemoration of the Declaration published at the Cross by Richard Cameron, on the

---

[1] The recorded reprieve of the Wigtown women is contained in a volume of the Register fairly written, and in excellent condition It can be *proved* that it was a *bound volume* when Wodrow got access to it, although the binding has been renewed in later times By his own showing, Wodrow had access to it, and remained in Edinburgh "looking over" these records, *before* he had written his romance of the Wigtown martyrs. Moreover, it can be proved, from his own History, that he *consulted*, and *quoted*, the registered proceedings of the Privy Council of 30th April 1685 (the date of the reprieve), in reference to another matter than the reprieve, and in illustration of a section of his History which occurs *before* the section containing his romance See note on this subject in " Memorials of Dundee," vol. ii. p 77.

twenty-second June 1680." Upon this memorable occasion, Professor Blackie blazed off like a rocket of Greek-fire, and we may believe their zealous chronicler when he says—" The learned Professor of Greek in the University of Edinburgh, standing on the broken wall of a crumbling feudal fortress, discoursing on the men of the Covenant to the people of Nithsdale, was a *unique* and interesting sight." But the speech of the occasion was from a gentleman holding her Majesty's commission: " Colonel Shaw of Ayr, having been introduced by Provost Whigham," said—" He read of Claverhouse, and he wanted words to express the *loathing and contempt* he entertained for that *miserable military scavenger*, who was *no soldier and no gentleman*. He could not *dip his tongue in a cesspool vile and filthy enough to paint his character*. As respects Claverhouse and Charles II., he might say, like master like man ; for the King was the vile slave of his own lusts, a *miserable brothel-keeper*, who ought not to have been allowed to live, but should have been *strangled at his birth*." Here is language more " delirious " than any used by us in " Memorials of Dundee," or by Principal Tulloch in Macmillan's Magazine. This hideous, but in our day harmless, raising of the ghost of the treasonable and truculent " Sanquhar Declaration," reminds one of a turnip-lantern spectre in a country kirk-yard. But it exhibits at once the type, and the far-reaching poison in Scotland, of Shields' " Hind Let Loose," and Wodrow's History.

SECTION IV.

How the Romance of the drowning of the Women at Wigtown was first concocted in the Parish of Kirkinner, in Galloway, and recorded by its Kirk-Session.

The idea of promulgating violent and false accusations against the fallen dynasty, by the parochial system of collecting sufferings, had, as we have seen, been adopted for some years before Wodrow was installed receiver-general thereof, and grand martyrologist for Scotland. The system was not original with the Presbyterian ministers of 1710. Their prototypes were *Napthali*, and *A Hind Let Loose*, and also that class of bitter pamphleteers who came out in shoals at the dawn of the Orange dynasty, which was their brightest sunshine. It is to such sources that Wodrow's disreputable friend, and London correspondent, George Ridpath, refers him, for the basis of his history, in a letter containing the following advice:—" I need not hint, that there are *great helps* to be had in the *Apologetical Relation; Napthali;* the *True Nonconformists; Jus Populi;* the *Hind Let Loose;* and other accounts of those named *Cameronians;* though the latter should be touched with great caution." The parochial process of collecting was ingenious and certain of success. Starting with the postulate, that the Governments of the Restoration had followed one undeviating course and progress of injustice, oppression, and cruelty, opposed to patriotic integrity, Christian sanctity, and rural innocence, every statement or story was at once received, and adopted for truth, whatever the source, if only it were sufficiently defamatory to illustrate with effect the great mother calumny. Accordingly, the ladle was sent round all the " suffering " parishes, by order of the tribunals of the Kirk, collecting this species of contribution chiefly from aged men and women, who were invalids and paupers. But all were expected to contribute a suffering, however small, to this grand *commination* against the fallen dynasty The head-collector was the minister of the parish What old mumper could withstand the minister ? Out of blindness, deafness, doitedness, crabbedness, and coughing, he extracted (inspired by zeal in the cause), whatever he wanted, and cooked it as he fancied. If ever there was a device better suited than another for promoting a system of false and calumnious history, it was this universal and hasty raking of all the common sewers of fanaticism for the discovery of some unknown quantity of sufferings. We must limit our illustrations of the *modus operandi* to instances afforded by the records of two neighbouring parishes. But they are very germain to the matter in hand, the one being *Kirkinner*, the parish of *old* Margaret

Lauchlison, the other *Penninghame*, the parish of *dear* Margaret Wilson, both in the county of Wigtown. In the original Session-book of the parish of Kirkinner, now preserved in the General Register House, we discovered the following instructive passages, which had hitherto escaped observation :—

"Januarie 15, 1710 —There being a *generall design throw the nation*,[1] to have a history of the late sufferings of the *People of God*, and every Session within this national Church being *desired* to gett *weel attested* informations of the *godly's sufferings* within their bounds, which each Session is to record, extract, and carry in the extract to the Presbyterie ; it's recommended to each member to *gather* and *prepare* their best informations of these things *against our next.* Sederunt closed with prayer "

The next entry on the subject is just *twenty-one days* thereafter ; not very ample time, one would think, to " gather and prepare well attested informations " of the godly's sufferings within their bounds. However, here it is :—

" Februarie 5, 1710 —Ane account of the sufferings of *honest people* in this paroch was *given in and read* If there be *anything to add*, the several members are to inform themselves, and then all is to be recorded together, that the Presbyterie may have an attested extract of all."

The grand result does not appear on this record until more than a whole twelvemonth after the above notices. Having examined the Kirkinner register very carefully, we can affirm there is no mistake as to dates. " January 15, 1710," is the date of the first recommendation to " gather and prepare," and this to be done " against our next." The next sederunt of the Session is, " February 5, 1710 ," at which time " an account is given in and read," but nothing recorded, the order being for a *renewed search.* The sederunts, of the register for this year, run on to the last, held, " November 27, 1710." Then come the sederunts of January 14, February 15, March 18, of the following year 1711 The next sederunt is " April 15, 1711," when the collected sufferings are for the first time *recorded.* And now old *Margaret Lauchlison* at last comes to the surface, and is tabled as a martyr. Her case forms the

---

[1] A very false mode of putting it The design was only general among the Presbyterian ministers.

leading and most important of Kirkinner's *gathered and prepared* sufferings, and is thus recorded :—

" Aprile 15, 1711 —*The minister* gave in the account of the sufferings of honest godly people, in the *late times,* which was read, and is as follows :—

" *Margaret Laughlison,* of known integrity and piety from her youth, aged about *eighty,*[1] widow of John Millikin, wright in Drumjargan, was, *in or about* the year of God 1685, in her own house taken off her knees in prayer, and carried immediatly to prison, and from one prison to another, without the benefit of light to read the Scriptures, was barbarously treated *by dragoons,* who were sent to carry her from Machirmore to Wigtoun, and being sentenced by *Sir Robert Grier of Lagg* to be drowned att a stake within the flood-mark, just below the town of Wigtoun, for *conventicle keeping and alledged rebellion,* was, *according to the said sentence,* fixed to the stake till the tide made, and *held down within the water by one of the town officers,* by his halbert at her throat, till she died."

This account, which has hitherto remained entirely latent, won't suit the worshippers of the Wigtown Martyrs. The " young maiden of eighteen," *Margaret Wilson,* the *Prima Donna* of that water-opera, is *not there!* This is not Wodrow's story; not Lord Macaulay's story, not the story that the world has. The minister had taken more than a whole twelvemonth to " gather and prepare" this story, and lo! it is *not the story.* Where is " *dear* Margaret Wilson," with her bible, and her psalm-book, and her pretty, graceful, winning, " edifying" ways? Had the minister of Kirkinner, in a twelvemonth's time, gathered nothing about her? Or having *gathered* the story in all the fulness of its rich details, had he *prepared* this finest tragedy of the troubles, the very Hamlet of our Martyrologies, so stupidly as to *omit the part of Ophelia?* But let us see how they pretend to verify this mutilated martyrdom.

To the *drowning* suffering, the leading and most extraordinary case in this Kirkinner catalogue, no attestation whatever is specially attached. But of this suffering, *inter alia,* " the minister gave in the account." What manner of man this minister was, and what manner of men practically composed

---

[1] Her own petition, of which these gatherers and preparers were *utterly ignorant,* gives her age as " *about* three score and ten."

this parochial kirk-session, or really had to do with this rude entry, no man alive can tell, though some may guess [1] The fact that it was a *minister* and a *kirk-session* of the garden of Scotch martyrologies, in the year 1710, who agreed to hold this record *for the truth*, may cast suspicion upon it, but can afford no proof. The character of such Presbyterial tribunals at that period, dealing with such stories for such a purpose, will only be accounted a sufficient voucher by those who are nervously anxious that such stories should not be proved false, or who are altogether uninformed as to the ways and means of Presbyterian government and dictation in those days. *Where or how* the minister got this rambling story of Margaret Lauchlison, is not said. No other or more precise record of the facts is referred to. No formal precognition is recorded, or pretended to have been taken. No certificate, or information by any eye-witness, is pretended to be forthcoming. But the *whole list* given in by the minister is *generally* approved of, and formally attested, by the following entry in the record, of that same date,—which attestation is as careful as possible *not to particularize* in the application :—

" The which *particulars aforesaid* being read, they [the Kirk-session], *partly* from *credible information*, *partly* from their own *personal knowledge*, doe *belive* the said *informations* to be *matter of fact*, and appoint the same to be recorded in their Session-book, *ad futuram rei memoriam*, and the clerk is to give *extract* to the Presbyterie of Wigtoun, according to appointment. Sederunt closed with prayer "

But attest, or believe, as they might, their " matter of fact," as regards Margaret Lauchlison at least, was *not* matter of fact. She was *not* sentenced for " conventicle keeping," but for refusing to take the Oath of Abjuration. She may have been *sentenced* by Sir Robert Grierson of Lagg, sitting along with at least two other Lords Commissioners at Wigtown ; but it is *not true*, what the minister's story clearly imports, that the old woman was forthwith taken and drowned " according to the said sentence." Of that accusation Sir Robert Grierson is fully acquitted *by the old woman herself.* Between her

---

[1] Dr Tulloch, in his article in Macmillan's Magazine, bestows a very high character upon them, *for the nonce* We would like to know how that character is verified

sentence, and whatever mode of release from this world's cares it pleased God finally to bestow upon her, there occurred her petition to the Privy Council, her transmission to Edinburgh her taking the Oath of Abjuration, and her consequent *pardon*. Dr Tulloch's device of a *subsequent* "high-handed outrage by provincial agents," won't save this kirk-session. The *town-officer and his halbert*, in that minister's story, is there referred to as part of the machinery of the *Executive*, in a case where tyrannical judgment was immediately followed by merciless execution. The proved facts, of the petition and pardon, and the violent theory of *lynch-law* by some *officials of the Government*, manifestly had never entered either the knowledge, or the imagination, of this minister or his session. They meant to record a Government prosecution, a judicial condemnation, and a Government execution. Now, from whatever source *gathered*, by whatever hand *prepared*, the Kirk-session of Kirkinner thereby stand convicted of having solemnly attested for truth, "*in perpetuam rei memoriam*," and sealed with prayer, an *abominable falsehood*.

SECTION V.

How the Romance of the Drowning of the Women at Wigtown was expanded into its present dimensions for the first time in the Session-book of the Parish of Penninghame

Wodrow makes no reference to the Session-book of Kirkinner, or to its minister. But he tells us:—"I shall mostly give my narrative of it" (the martyrdom in question), "from *an account* I have from the fore-mentioned Mr Rowan, *now with the Lord*, late minister of *Penninghame*, where Margaret Wilson lived, who was at pains to have its circumstances fully vouched by witnesses, *whose attestations are in my hands*." This jesuitical mode of stating his authorities, extremely characteristic of Wodrow, means no more than this, that he had obtained an extract, certified by Mr Rowan, acting as clerk, from the Session-book of *Penninghame*, of precisely the same kind and character as that which we have quoted from *Kirkinner*, except that, in Mr Rowan's hands, the melo-dramatic tragedy had become fully developed in all its martyrological glory. This Session-book is still preserved in the parish of Penninghame, not having been removed to the Register House in Edinburgh, where that of Kirkinner now is. There was printed, however, at Newton-Stewart, in 1826, "Extract from the Session-book of the parish of Penninghame." This contains, *inter alia*, a long history, domestic and martyrological, of the two Wigtown sufferers, but more especially of the family and sufferings of the "maiden of eighteen," whom the minister of Kirkinner had failed to find, or, more strangely still, had omitted to notice. We learn from Wodrow that the Penninghame story was gathered and prepared by his friend Mr Robert Rowan, minister of that parish, who primed him therewith for his own history of the martyrdom. Having no reason to doubt that the Newton-Stewart publication is a faithful and accurate transcript from the original record, we shall give it here as the *Penninghame* version, which Wodrow had transferred to his pages very nearly *verbatim*. The following minute of Session, dated 15th February 1711 (as extracted in the Newton-Stewart print), discloses the instructions upon which the parish minister had proceeded :—

" The General Assembly, and then Commission, having recommended it to Presbyteries, to cause an exact account of the sufferings of people in every paroch, for their adherence to the *covenanted work of reformation*, in opposition to the late *Erastian Prelacy*, to be collected by Sessions, with the best documents and attestation of them that can be had by the respective Sessions, and the Presbytery having frequently recommended the same,—the minister presented a collection of the *sufferings* given up to him by *the persons best acquainted with them*, which being read, the Session informs of *several material things that are wanting*, and orders them to be insert and presented. *Sederunt* closed with prayer."

It would appear that, upon this occasion, too, the minister had been sent to *try again*, and that accordingly he had produced a second batch, which was added to the former; and then, on the 25th February 1711, the following is minuted :—

" The particulars that *were wanting*, in the account of the sufferings of people under the late Prelacy, *being insert in the former account*, all was produced and read. the tenor whereof follows."

After a variety of less important sufferings with which the record commences, we come to that destined to constitute the very pink of Scotch martyrology :—

" Gilbert Wilson in Glenvernoch, in Castlestewart's land, being a man to *ane excesse conform* to the guise of the tymes, and his wife *without challenge for her religion,* in a good condition as to worldly things, with a great stock on a large ground (*fitt to be a prey*), was harassed *for his children* who *would not conform* They being required to take the test, and hear the Curats, refused both, were searched for, fled, and lived in the wild mountains, bogs, and caves. Their parents were charged on their highest peril, that they should neither *harbour them, speak, supplie them, nor see them ;* and the contrey people were obliged by the terror of the laws, to pursue them, as weal as the souldiers, with *hue and cry* "

" In February 1685, Thomas Wilson, of *sixteen years of age,* Margaret Wilson of *eighteen years,* Agnes Wilson of *thirteen years,* children to the said Gilbert: The said Thomas, keeping the mountains, his two sisters, Margaret and Agnes, went *secretly to* Wigtoun to see some friends, were there discovered, taken prisoners, and *instantly thrust into the thieves hole,* as the greatest malefactors, whence they were sometymes brought up to the Tolbooth after a considerable tyme's imprisonment, where several others were prisoners for the like causes Particularly ane *Margaret M'Lachland of Kirkinner paroch,* a woman of sixty-three years of age

" After their imprisonment for some considerable tyme, Mr David Graham Shireff, the Laird of Lagg, Major Winram, Captain Strachan, called ane assize, indicted these *three women,* viz. Margaret M'Lauchland, Margaret Wilson, Agnes Wilson, to be guilty of the *Rebellion at Bothwell-bridge, Airds-mosse, twenty field conventicles,* and *twenty house conventicles .* Yet it was weel known that none of these *women* ever were within twenty miles of Bothwell, or Airds-mosse ; and *Agnes* Wilson, being *eight years of age* at the time of Airds-mosse, could not be deep in rebellion then , nor her sister of *thirteen* years of age, and *twelve* years at Bothwell Bridge its tyme. The assize did sit, and brought them in guilty, and the Judges sentenced them to be tyed to palisados fixed in the sand, within the flood mark of the sea, and there to stand till the flood overflowed them, and drowned them

" They received their sentence without the least discouragement, with a *composed smiling countenance,* judging it their honour to suffer for Christ's Truth, that he is alone King and Head of his Church. Gilbert Wilson forsaid got his youngest daughter, *Agnes Wilson,* out of prison, upon his bond of *ane hundreth pounds sterling* to produce her when called for, *after the sentence of death passed against* her , but was obliged to go to Edinburgh for this before it could be obtained The time they were in prison, no means were unessayed with *Margaret Wilson* to persuade her to take the Oath of Abjuration, and *hear the Curats,* with threaten-ings and flattery, but *without any success.*

" Upon the 11th day of May, 1685, these *two women,* Margaret M'Lachland and Margaret Wilson, were brought forth to execution

They did put the old woman first into the water, and when the water was overflowing her, they asked Margaret Wilson what she thought of her in that case? She answered, 'What do I see but Christ wrestling there, think ye that we are the sufferers? No, it is Christ in us, for he sends none a warfare on their own charges' Margaret Wilson sang psalm 25, from the 7th verse, red the 8th chapter of the Epistle to the Romans, and did pray, and then *the water covered her* But before her breath was quite gone, they pulled her up, and held her till she could speak, and then asked her if she would pray for the King? She answered, that *she wished the salvation of all men, but the damnation of none* Some of her *relations* being on the place, cried out, '*She is willing to conform,*'—being desirous to save her life at any rate. Upon which *Major Winram offered the Oath of Abjuration to her*, either to swear it, or to return to the water She refused it, saying,—'*I will not, I am one of Christ's children, let me go*' And then they returned her into the water, being a virgin martyr of *eighteen* years of age, suffering death for her refusing to swear the Oath of Abjuration, and *hear the Curates.*

"The said Gilbert Wilson was fined for the *opinion of his children*, harassed with frequent quarterings of souldiers upon him, sometimes ane hundieth men at once, who lived at discretion on his goods, and that for *several years together*, and his frequent attendance on the Courts at Wigtown, almost every week, at thirteen miles distance, *for three years time*, riding to Edinburgh on these accounts, so that his losses could not be reckoned, and estimat (without doubt) not within five thousand merks; yet for *no principle or action or actions of his own*, and died in great poverty lately. A few years hence, his wife, a very aged woman, lived upon the charity of friends; his son, Thomas, lived to bear arms under King William, in Flanders, and the Castle of Edinburgh, but had nothing by his parents to enter the ground which they possessed, where he lives *to certifie the truth* of these things, with *many others* who know them too well."

To verify *specifically* this unique mixture of the marvellous, and the nonsensical, there is, as may well be supposed, not an attempt. But at the conclusion of the record, the *whole catalogue* of sufferings, has this *general* attestation applied to it:—

"The Session having considered *all the above particulars*, and having certain knowledge of the truth of the *most part of them*, from their own *sufferings*, and eye-witnesses of the foresaid sufferings *of others*, which several of the Session *declares*, and from certain information of *others*, in the very tyme and place they were acted in, and many living that have *all these things* fresh in their memory; except of these things concerning Gilbert Milroy, the truth whereof *they think* there is no ground to doubt of They do *attest* the same, and ordeis ane extract to be given in their name to the Presbytery, to transmit to superior Judicatories. *Sederunt closed with prayer.*" [1]

----

[1] This Penninghame record is entitled,—"A brief Information of the

The value, as an *attestation,* of this extraordinary specimen of fanatical mystification, we intend to bring to the test in a subsequent section. Meanwhile we may here point to it, as throwing some light upon that deceptive statement in Wodrow's narrative, that his friend the minister " was at pains to have the circumstances fully vouched by witnesses, *whose attestations are in my hands.*" Nothing of the kind is to be found in any volume of Wodrow's collections. Manifestly this means neither more nor less than the *general attestation* at the conclusion of the Session record, which, so far from being an " attestation by witnesses," has not even a special reference, *quantum valeat,* to the drowning tragedy at Wigtown. If there were such attestations by eye-witnesses, we ask, *where are they,* and *who were the witnesses?* If there were any eye-witnesses at all, to that fearful scene, there must have been *hundreds.* Was there *not one,* then, to attest it to the reverend David Williamson, who was collecting such sufferings *immediately after the event?*

Wodrow, justly suspicious that his narrative may not be credited, gives some account of the rebel wanderings, in after life, of young Thomas Wilson; and adds, that he " *lives now in his father's room, and is ready to attest all I am writing*" But we are by no means prepared to admit that Thomas Wilson really *was ready to attest* any thing at all, merely because Wodrow is so bold as to say so in his loose and jesuitical manner. The Session record had phrased it more cautiously,— " where he lives *to certifie* the truth of these things,"—the *precise things,* not being specified. It is not easy to appreciate the extent, or value of an attestation that was *never made.* But even supposing that the Orange rebel, as Wodrow describes him, had actually attested the fate of his sister as nar-

---

sufferings of people which are most remarkable in the parish of Peninghame, within the shire of Wigtown, upon the account of their adherence to the Reformation of the Church of Scotland, and their refusing to conform with Prelacie, with the occasions of their trouble, especiallie from the year 1679 to the year 1689." It will be seen that these *collectors* in the year 1711, are just imitators of the collectors in 1687, whose papers we disclosed in Part I. (see before pp. 64-68), and none of which papers contain any notice whatever of this wonderful Wigtown martyrdom in 1685.

rated by the martyrologist, it would just come to this, that Thomas Wilson had attested for truth that which is *proved to be false*, as did the Kirk-sessions of Kirkinner and Penninghame.

SECTION VI

Principal Tulloch's Theory of Embellishments.

Dr Tulloch speaks of this story having been told " with a rude but touching *picturesqueness* by Wodrow;" and, " by Lord Macaulay in our own day in one of the most graphic and impressive passages of his History of England." But neither of these authors have the slightest merit in the composition, if any merit there be. Lord Macaulay's impressive passage is just a garbled extract from Wodrow; and Wodrow's " picturesqueness" is just a *verbatim* extract from the Session-book of Penninghame, given him by the minister. It is of more importance to observe, however, that we have taught the Chair of St Andrews University to see, and even brought it to say, that, picturesque or grotesque, Wodrow's story is *not true*. Mark how, *me ipso duce*, the Head of St Mary's demolishes both Wodrow and Macaulay, and martyrologies in general, in the following passage of the Macmillan philippic :—

" Such is the well-known Wigtown martyrology [1] Like many other martyrologies, it has *evidently* [2] been surrounded with a *considerable portion of fictitious embellishment* It is not likely that the martyr scene was so *entirely edifying* as represented in the pages of Wodrow. The picturesque adjuncts surrounding the young sufferer—the ' maiden of eighteen '—are plainly touched by the imaginative pathos that grows *naturally* out of any such time of Christian suffering and persecution Every one who knows any thing of martyrologies, knows how inevitably they gather to themselves such picturesque touches, and especially *such*

---

[1] May we take the liberty to suggest that it is a *martyrdom*, not a *martyrology* ?

[2] How long has this been considered evident ? "

pieces of edifying discourse as the sayings attributed to Margaret Wilson.[1] There is not a martyrology in the early Church—to take the purest examples—that does not present something of the same phenomena. Who believes that the martyrdom of Polycarp, or of the Lyonnese martyrs, or of the Carthagenian maiden Perpetua, happened exactly as they have been depicted to us by Church tradition? All who study these *beautiful old stories*, with any critical eye, are forced at once to allow the *admixture* of picturesque and edifying matter they contain It is the *rule* of this sort of literature to become impregnated in its descent by the *imaginative fertility* of the *consciousness of the time*, and still more, of the immediately succeeding time, which learns to look back with a reverend wonder and love to the tragic events which made heroic the former days The Wigtown martyrology is certainly no exception to this rule Wodrow's stories *everywhere bear the stamp of this imaginative development.* But are Wodrow and his authorities therefore *liars;* and the Wigtown martyrology a mere imposture from beginning to end—a calumnious fable, as it has been *politely* termed? Were the two women *never at all* drowned at Wigtown?"

Must we also submit to have dust thrown in our eyes from the ruins of our once famous St Andrews after this fashion? Never mind Polycarp and the Carthagenian maiden Perpetua. A truce with those " beautiful old stories." The story of Margaret Wilson is just as beautiful, but it will not be our fault if it ever live to be as old. We answer that last question in the affirmative. *Yes*—the two women were drowned at Wigtown, never at all, at all. We said, and do say, that it is a *calumnious fable* from beginning to end. But we never said so until we had *proved* it. It is the polished Principal who speaks of " liars." Give us our own language, at least, bad as it is. Wodrow was a muddle-headed Scotch martyrologist, imposing upon himself, easily imposed upon by others in such matters, and ever willing to be so. Thus he came to impose upon Scotland. Our Doctor of Divinity, however, has at last discovered that Wodrow's story of this martyrdom " has *evidently* been surrounded with a *considerable* amount of *fictitious embellishment.*" But that is not all Wodrow's doing. It appertains to the Penninghame Session-book, and to the accusing spirit that " gave it in," and the recording angel that wrote it down. And if the fictitious character of the story

---

[1] The worshippers of the Wigtown martyrs won't thank the Principal for such support as this against " Memorials of Dundee."

was also *evident* to Lord Macaulay (as, according to Dr Tulloch, it *ought* to have been,) then had that great author sacrificed the integrity of history to a bit of miserable clap-trap, which he had neither the merit of composing, nor the excuse of believing. Well then. There *are* "fictitious embellishments" clinging to this martyrdom, but no more of a destructive quality than the graceful creepers that serve to keep an old tree cosy. They are, indeed, a subsequent growth, but a growth natural to the tree itself, like the verdant suckers of a glorious ash. This is curious, however, that when we recur to the period immediately before that when the natural embellishments may be understood to have commenced to spring, the stem they are supposed to embellish disappears altogether! In 1687 these embellishments did not exist. Certainly not, says Dr Tulloch, because "the consciousness of the immediate succeeding time" had not yet "learnt to look back with a reverent wonder and love to the tragic event which made heroic the former days" Brave words. But will the eloquent Presbyterian Professor undertake to show us this virgin sacrifice in its pristine purity—the *truth*, naked and unadorned, without a figment or a fig-leaf of embellishment? "Dainty Davie," according to Dr Tulloch's theory, was too close upon the event to command its *natural embellishments*. But how came he to be ignorant of *the thing embellished*?

Nevertheless, our learned censor lays great stress upon this embellished fable being "a tradition which has lived *universally in the hearts* of the peasantry of Galloway since the commencement of the last century" Here, too, we have eloquent verbiage, but neither proof nor argument. This "universality in peasant hearts" is an idea as fanciful as the language in which it is clothed, and more easily said than proved. The martyrdom of Little Red Ridinghood also enjoys that sort of universal life in *congenial* hearts. Who cared to test or impugn Wodrow? But there were other hearts in Scotland above the influence which then ruled the peasant's heart, that refused to admit the truth of that so-called *tradition*. Dr Tulloch forgets that when Wodrow and Kirk-sessions were busy with this martyrdom, at the commencement of the last century, the martyrologist had to work, as he himself admits, against a *denial of the fact;* a denial "impudently" asserted "by the advocates for the cruelty of this period, and our Jacobites." He forgets, too, that when Patrick Walker, years afterwards, published his insane variety of the martyrdom, he also declared it to be one "*which some deny to be matter of fact.*" The vulgar reception and embellishing of the fable in certain districts of Scotland, its poetical adaptation by lovers of the romance of religion, or its careless adoption by uninquisitive minds, may be common enough. But its *universality*, as a proper *ab initio* traditionary belief, is an unwarrantable assumption, a fallacy, and a myth. Even the bare fact of the *drowning* was unknown in the century before last, when, if true, it must have been best known.

With evident self-complacency the Doctor parades his elaborate and original theory, that embellishments, and it would seem to any amount, are not only the natural produce, but the proper exponent, of a *true* martyrdom. "Its embellishments," he says, "as *told by Wodrow*, are *natural developments*, supposing a *basis of fact* granted; but the natural imaginative process which sufficiently accounts for these embellishments, could never create the fact, supposing it to be absolutely without foundation." Again, he says:—"*Admit* the fact of the drowning, the kirk-session records are perfectly intelligible; their *edifying exaggerations* are only the *natural halo* which the fact would gather round it; but *deny* the fact of the drowning and the whole story becomes a marvellous and incredible mass of invention." We are not to be caught by this logical coaxing, if logic it be Granted, "embellishments" pre-suppose *something* embellished. But it does not follow that this something must be precisely the thing that Dr Tulloch desiderates. We cannot discover that the "edifying exaggerations of the kirk-session records" are of such a nature, however edifying, as distinctly to indicate that the actual thing exaggerated is a *martyrdom* of these two women. One kirk-session records it in the form of a solitary old woman held down in the water by a solitary burgh-officer, armed with the lethal insignia of his office and authority. Another kirk-session, about the same time, and in the very same district, introduces *two* martyrs on the tragic scene, surrounded by lavish decorations, of scenery and dresses, the one previously omitted being by far the most interesting character, and destined in future to play the principal part—the "maiden of eighteen." Next, we have Wodrow introducing a *third* female on the stage, one still more interesting, being a child "not thirteen years of age," arraigned for high treason with the others, condemned with the others to be tied to a stake until drowned by the tide of the Solway, and only not drowned with the others per favour of the martyrologist not carrying that "edifying exaggeration" any further. Was the maiden martyr a natural embellishment emanating from the fact of the old martyr? Or was the child a natural embellishment growing out of the fact of the other two? What is the true thing that was embellished? We are forcibly reminded, by all this, of another well-known legend, not quite so old as Polycarp, that of the atrabilarious subject, namely, who vomited something as "black as a crow," and then, through an arithmetical progression of "edifying exaggerations," became immortalized as that marvellous martyr to bile, who brought up three black crows in full plumage It has never been thought in this case, that the imaginative progression of the crows, even had the increase been carried to three hundred, was utterly inexplicable, unless the disgorging of one crow, for a "basis of fact," were admitted, as some reasoner might have desiderated. But Dr Tulloch must forgive one of the Dundreary school of logic for going slowly and gingerly over that logical ground of his once more. The thing embellished being *true*, it is easy to understand and account for any *false* embellishments. That is a natural halo of falsehood emanating from truth. But if we are to suppose the thing embellished to be as false as the embellishing thing, then the Professor is nonplust. Is that it? Poor "dear Margaret Wilson!" She was *drowned* to be sure. Without that basis of fact she could not have been embellished. But alas! the bright crown of her martyrdom, so long worshipped in Scotland, has been resolved into a *Will-o'-the-Wisp* by the Primarius Professor of Divinity at St Andrews! It is nothing but "a halo" of false embellishments!

Of what earthly, or heavenly, use to the Calendar of the

Covenant, is the bare fact of the drowning? What the Covenant insists for is a *martyrdom*, and a martyrdom perpetrated
by the *Government of the Restoration.* Now if these women,
instead of being executed in immediate fulfilment of their sentence (which is the *only* version of their tragedy that has ever
come to us, either from tradition, Kirk-sessions, or Orange
chroniclers), were reprieved and pardoned by the Government
under which they were condemned,—a state of the case which
is *proved*, and which Dr Tulloch concedes,—the *martyrdom* is
gone. And if the more modern theory, of their having been
lynched nevertheless, in the face of hundreds of their zealous
friends, by a few murderous " official agents," acting *against*
the mercy of the Government and the Crown, and never called
to account for that rebellious deed, of which not a shadow of a
record is anywhere to be found,—if, we say, the slightest re-
flection of an intelligent mind must come to the conclusion that
this supplementary theory is the mere *straw-catching* struggles
of a convicted calumny, and bears the stamp of *nonsense* on the
very face of it.—then the *murder* is gone too! What remains?
An *accidental* drowning, by local officials " carrying out the
sentence which they *did not know* had been reprieved? This
is not even Wodrow's supplementary theory. It dates no further back than newspaper scribbling subsequent to the publication of " Memorials of Dundee." We have now shown it to
be impossible It is impossible, under all the circumstances,
that the fact of a reprieve recorded in Edinburgh on the 30th
of April was unknown on the 11th of May at Wigtown, supposing the women to have been there awaiting the result of
the efforts to save them. Moreover, by the 11th of May there
was no existing sentence against them capable of being acci-
dentally " carried out." The assumed error in the *record* of
the reprieve—*Edinburgh* for *Wigtown*—has nothing whatever
to do with the question of the fact of the reprieve having
reached Wigtown. Dr Tulloch has not taken up the *accident*
theory, although he says that the simple question to be solved,
is—" Were these women really drowned or not?" But that is
not the question. The question, truly, is this: Were these
women *officially drowned at Wigtown*, under a show, at least,
of *Government authority and support*, whether by the regular

act of the Government, constituting a *martyrdom;* or by a cruel outrage on the part of Government local agents, constituting a *murder;* or by a blunder of the Executive, belonging to the chapter of *accidents?* Now, each and all of these alternatives have been disproved beyond the reach of rational contradiction. Not one of them can be taken to furnish Dr Tulloch's postulate of a "basis of fact." An *official drowning,* under any of the three above categories, is totally out of the question. But they have all been mooted in their turn. Then they all must resolve into "embellishments," growing out of some other basis of fact. What, then, are we to grant now? What will satisfy the Professor's postulate, and relieve him from the predicament he seems to dread of being utterly nonplust? "Admit the women to have been *drowned:*"—"Admit the fact of the *drowning,*"—he pleads, piteously. If I admit the drowning, Doctor, call me a "soused gurnet," settle the embellishments as you may.

And is the logic of St Mary's so commanding, and infallible, as to oblige us to "admit the fact of the drowning," in the face of irresistible evidence that the women *were not drowned?* Must we admit it in the face of proof that they were *reprieved and pardoned?* In the face of proof that they were alive in Edinburgh at the very time they are said to have been drowned at Wigtown? In the face of the negative evidence of the Burgh Records of Wigtown, that no such execution had occurred there? In the face of proof that both did take the Abjuration Oath, at Edinburgh, for refusing to take which, with "an enthusiasm" (says Lord Macaulay) "as lofty as any that is recorded in martyrology," Margaret Wilson is figured to have been drowned in the Solway? In the face of the fact, that Sir George Mackenzie, the Lord Advocate, emphatically declared the reign of James II. in Scotland to be innocent of the execution of any State criminal of the female sex, by any form of death whatsoever? In the face of the fact that the Cameronian pamphleteer, who answered Sir George in detail, tacitly admitted that particular statement? In the face of the fact that that statement is negatively confirmed by Fountainhall? In the face of the fact that that statement is *exactly corroborated* by the Cameronian accusations of cruelty, in executing women, contained in various papers, framed by the bitterest opponents of Government in aid of the Orange invasion? In the face of the fact that every authentic record of their proceedings evinces the greatest anxiety on the part of the Government to exercise forbearance towards State criminals of the female sex? In the face of the fact that neither record, nor journal, nor letter, public or private, of the period, affords a trace of these women having been put to death? Depend upon it, Doctor, the *drowning,* too, is an *embellishment,* unless it be they drowned themselves.

But can we not find another " basis of fact," that will dispense with the drowning in that quality? Both these women, with the true spirit of Scotch Martyrs, refused to take the Abjuration Oath. For this fanatical obstinacy, *coram publico,* they were remitted to a jury, and condemned to die *by drowning.* That it was a very sad scene, a lamentable display of ignorant, misguided fanaticism, occurring in the midst of much popular excitement, and many humane attempts to bring the poor women to their senses, we have no manner of doubt. *There* is the real " basis of fact." That satisfies the Principal's postulate. The *drowning* is not the *thing embellished;* it is only the chief *embellishing thing.*

SECTION VII.

An Alibi proved for the Provost of Wigtown against the Evidence of the Ghost of old Margaret Lauchlison.

Among those whom Wodrow libels as prominently engaged in the martyrdom, or the *lynching,* of these two women, is William Coltran of Drummoral, who was Provost of Wigtown in that year 1685. The martyrologist, through one of his numerous clerical correspondents, had learnt, late in the year 1717, that one *Elizabeth Milliken,* said to be a daughter of the *old* saint, Margaret Lauchlison, was still living in the parish of Kirkinner, herself now aged, maimed, and a pauper. Moreover, that, in the year 1708, this old woman had *dreamed a dream,* which the minister of Kirkinner had failed to gather, in 1711, but which was very germain to the matter of the Wigtown martyrdom, and brought Heaven itself to witness against Provost Coltran. Wodrow, the keenest nose in Scotland for a kirk miracle, quests it out forthwith. He puts himself into communication with the then minister of Kirkinner, one Mr William Campbell, and is in due time "refreshed" with the following reply, dated 11th April 1718 :—

"R D B [Reverend and Dear Brother],—I'm particularly refreshed to understand from Mr Miller that you'r weel. In compliance with your desire anent Elizabeth Millikin's dream, know that I went and discoursed her this day, in order to give you the genuine account of it. The said Elizabeth dreamed, some weeks or months before the Quarter Sessions that met in November 1708, that her mother, Margaret Lauchlison, came to her, at the Cross of Wigton, with garb, gesture, and countenance that she had five minutes before she was drowned in Blednoch, and said to her, '*Elizabeth, go and warn Provost Cultran that he must shortly compear before the tribunal of the great God, to answer for his ways,*' and immediately her sleep was broken, and it made such an impression upon her, that she resolved, for her own exoneration, and the Provost's edification, prudently and meekly to communicate the said dream to the said William Cultran of Drummorral, with the first convenience, but not finding or expecting that, she told the dream to Bailie Lafries, Drummorral's friend—being married to Lady Drummorral's sister—a man of age, gravity, and experience, and an elder in Wigton ; and solemnly desired and engaged him to signify the said dream to the said Drummorral, and she doubted not but the said Bailie Lafries did tell the said Drummorral. And, *accordingly*, in the beginning of November 1708, he rode from Wigton to the Quarter Session of the Justices of the shire, that met that time at Stranraer, and there, on the Wednesday, at the Court table, was suddenly struck with a lethargy, was carried to his quarters, and continued speechless till Saturday the 8th of November, and then died."

This important communication had induced Wodrow to write again, but the rejoinder from his friend, dated Kirkinner, May 14, 1718, was not so satisfactory. The Rev. William Campbell then writes :—

"R. D. B —Next morning after I was favoured with yours, I *discoursed* Elizabeth Milliken, but she cannot give you farther satisfaction as to the circumstances of her dream ; only she dreamed it in her own bed, in the town of Barnbarroch, *and all the relations of Provost Coltran and Bailie Lafries deny they know anything of the Bailie's informing the Provost, or the Provost's answer.*"

It is material to know what manner of woman this dreamer

was, and fortunately that information is afforded in Mr Campbell's first letter :—

" The said Elizabeth is poor but pious; a widow indeed, *the worthy daughter of such a martyred mother.* It has pleased God lately to afflict her by a *sore fall* in her walking home from this church, and having a Bible under her arm, and falling with a great deal of violence upon that side where the Bible was, it has *broken some of her ribs,* and disables her for business I have been her acquaintance for sixteen years I know she is *poor and straitened,* but I never heard her say she wanted anything If ye please, procure, and send Mr Martin, bookseller in Edinburgh, some supply."

We would like to have cross-examined this old woman, or to have heard the precise mode in which the minister " discoursed" her on the subject. That he had done so with the belief strong in his own mind that the *martyrdom* of old Margaret Lauchlison was an incontrovertible fact, may be gathered from his own letter. But we now know that that assumed fact is a fable. Considering the maimed and aged state of this pauper, that her mother was actually drowned, as described in the Kirkinner Session-book of 1711, is a hallucination or confusion which she might very easily imbibe from her minister, who was assuming the fact, and much interested to have it embellished as a fact. If no more were known than what these letters disclose, then, even this second-hand evidence, from the daughter, referring to the " *garb, gesture,* and *countenance* that she (her mother) had five minutes before *she was drowned in Blednoch,*" would necessarily convey a belief, that here was the evidence of an *eye-witness,* who had the best *causa scientiæ,* and who could not be mistaken. But then, we now happen to know more than either the daughter or the minister who discoursed her seem to have known. We *know* that the Kirkinner record on the subject, of date seven years prior to this ministerial precognition of the old invalid, is a false record : false in fact, and calumnious in spirit, from whatever source derived. This hearsay evidence of 1718 stands on the same false footing. It is all based upon *ignorance of the facts,* that Margaret Lauchlison was allowed to petition for her life; that she petitioned the Privy Council to be allowed to take the Abjuration Oath; that she was removed to Edinburgh; that she there *did take* the Abjuration Oath, between the 13th and the 30th of April 1685, and was *pardoned* in consequence   These facts were utterly unknown to Wodrow (so he says himself), in 1718.   Manifestly, the minister of Kirkinner was in the same state of ignorance.   Then, what is the value of their research?   And what was the mental condition of this old maimed pauper, who could not *enlighten them* as to the *real history* of her own mother in so important a particular as her petition for life and consequent reprieve?

Let us try it by the formula of Dr Tulloch's theory of *embellishments*.   The *ghost* will at once be admitted an embellishment.   What is the " basis of fact " to which it forms the " natural halo?"   Of course, that Provost Coltran had been tyrannically conspicuous in the cruel martyrdom.   *Grant that*, and the ghost is easily accounted for as " a natural development."   *Deny that*, and the old woman's evidence " becomes a marvellous and utterly incredible mass of invention "   But it cannot be granted.   For it is now *proved*, that Provost Coltran was absent from Wigtown, and could not possibly have taken any part whatever in the sacrifice.   This fact is placed beyond question by the *Burgh Records of Wigtown* (already quoted in the first part of this investigation), where the following entry appears —

" Wigton, June 26, 1685 —Convened—the Provost, the two Bailies, [and twelve Councillors named]   The which day, William Coltrane, Provost, who was elected Commissioner to the Parliament, having *returned*, has made his report as follows, viz —that he was *seventy-three days absent*, and that he gave in three rex-dollars and ane half-dollar with his commission; and that he gave one dollar to Bartholomew M'Kean, for his reveiting to the town's papers—which , in haill, extends to the sum of two hundred twenty and four pounds and fifteen shillings Scots money, at ane rex dollar ilk day , conform to the former Act," &c

Now, if the Provost was absent for *seventy-three days prior* to 26th June, he must have been absent *at least* since the 14th of April *inclusive*, which was the day after the condemnation of the two women at Wigtown.   But this calculation assumes that the Town-Council held their sederunt (26th June, at which the Provost was present), and received his report, the very day after his return, which is not likely.   So, in all probability, he had been absent from Wigtown when the women were condemned, as well as upon the alleged day of their execution ; and certainly he was not on the Commission that tried them.

Provost Coltran being thus completely exonerated (for the first time during a century and a-half past), notwithstanding the testimony of the *ghost*, we have to seek for another " basis of fact." The *ghost story* might be (upon Dr Tulloch's principle), a natural false growth out of such a fact as that Provost Coltran had been conspicuous in the cruel tragedy. But that fact proving to be an embellishment also, it cannot, in its turn, be so easily accounted for as a *natural* false growth out of such a fact as that the women were drowned. The ghost lied. We are not bound to be *polite* to a ghost. Provost Coltran was at the scene of the *pardon*, and not of the *martyrdom*. Now, assuming it for the fact that my Lord Justice Lagg, and Captain-Lieutenant Winram of the Dragoons, took these pardoned women, and *ex proprio motu*, and in the face of a hostile and remonstrating mob, hunted them to death in the Blednoch as if they had been witches or water-fowl,—that Provost Coltran was a chief actor in that ploy, and was suddenly summoned to Heaven as a judgment therefor, is a ghostly embellishment which seems to have no natural affinity to the assumed fact. What between the ghost and the minister, the brain of this crushed old woman would seem to have been addled on the subject ; and, considering the *proved* facts of the case, her evidence, as reported, can lead to no other conclusion.

There happens to be, however, a *proved* " basis of fact" capable of accounting for all the embellishments, including both the ghost-story and the drowning, when derived from such a source as this unfortunate old pauper, *discoursed* by a martyrological minister begging the question. Her mother had been tried for high treason at Wigtown thirty-three years before, had been capitally convicted, and condemned to be drowned. The memory of that awful event, with all its necessary concomitants of fanatical excitement, persuasions, distress, and alarm, would doubtless still weigh upon the old woman's mind. With the *preliminary* history of the criminal, her arrest and imprisonment, the Provost of course would be officially concerned. That she had arrived at mercy through a stormy and dangerous passage cannot be doubted. In the Kirkinner Ses-

sion-book we find the following suggestive *item*, set down as a
" suffering " " William Karr in Borland, *anno* 1685, was *imprisoned with* the said Margaret Lauchlison, and *made his
escape.*" The old woman was *not drowned* But she had been
condemned to be drowned. There (again we say) is the real fact
of the 17th century. *All the rest* belongs to the " edifying
exaggerations of Kirk-session records," (the language is Dr
Tulloch's), and Kirk martyrologists, of the 18th century.

SECTION VIII

*That all the various versions of the Wigtown Romance are
manifestly based upon falsehood, contradictory of each
other, and incredible in themselves*

Having disposed of the theory of a martyrological " basis of
fact " surrounded by a " natural halo of false embellishments,"
let us now consider the case under the more intelligible aspect
of a basis of falsehood overlaid by a variety of incredible and
contradictory embellishments, according to the fancy of ignorant and unscrupulous embellishers.

There is not a variety of this martyrdom, from Alexander
Shields' " short hint " in 1690, to Wodrow's long calumny in
1722, that is not manifestly based on falsehood, *in essentialibus.*
One and all involve the statement, that these two women were
drowned at Wigtown on the 11th of May 1685, passing at
once, without a symptom of relenting, from a lawless sentence
to a barbarous execution. One and all are based upon the
assumption, that the Government of James II., in Scotland,
was a Government by savages, who spared neither sex, nor
age, nor childhood, nor piety, nor innocence, in their murderous decrees, and who were especially cruel and relentless in
their treatment of tender and saintly females, whom they *habitually* drowned " for their religion." And this, unquestionably
the basis of the Wigtown martyrdom, in all its varieties, is now
proved to be so intensely untrue, that to reconcile it with any-

thing but the most virulent spirit of calumnious falsehood, is purely impossible. And when we come to examine the details, of the different versions, of this fanatical imposition upon History,—this low-born libel upon all the best blood of Scotland,—we find them so incredible in themselves, and so contradictory of each other, that no reflecting mind can escape from the conclusion, that this is a gross case of falsehood heaped upon falsehood, and not a case of natural embellishment superinduced upon substantial facts.

The earliest version of the double martyrdom, in full bloom, is that recorded in the *Penninghame* Session-book. This we have given *in extenso* (pp. 102–3) from the published text of that record, which had been given out by the parish minister to Wodrow, for the purposes of his History. Part of this, the tit-bit, was culled, from Wodrow, by Lord Macaulay, nearly *verbatim*. But the noble historian was too wary to shake the credit of that clap-trap episode in his History of England, by also repeating, from Wodrow, the *incredible domestic history* of the family of the Wilsons, which the martyrologist also obtained from the Penninghame Session-book, in that extract given him by his friend Mr Rowan, the minister, who had *gathered* and *prepared* it. If ever a story bore the stamp of falsehood upon every line of it, we have it there. The father of these children, a substantial and wealthy farmer on the estate of a brother of the Earl of Galloway, was strictly, and by inclination, *Episcopalian*. He was not only a prudent *Conformist*, but, upon principle, he was of that persuasion "to ane excesse." His wife, the mother of these children, was of the same persuasion, being "without any challenge for her religion." No one of common intelligence, or of ordinary reading on the subject, could entertain a doubt that this character of the heads of a family in the year 1685 necessarily infers that they must have been in high favour with Government, under no suspicion or observation whatever, and as far as possible removed from the chance of persecution. But we are actually told that the *Posse Comitatus* was raised to support the *military*, " with hue and cry," in pursuit of the children of such parents, two of them females, as if they had been lions and tigers escaped from a menagerie. At the commencement of the year 1685 the Government were wholly intent upon the alarming prospect of Argyle's invasion Their great object of pursuit was armed conventicle outlaws, lurking and wandering about the west and south, with the view of ere long joining the invading army, and meanwhile exciting the people, waylaying the poor soldiers on duty, and murdering the loyal. As for hunting children for not " hearing curats," the Executive of 1685 would as soon have thought of hunting sparrows on the housetop. The Kirk-session story of the mental condition, the polemico-religious devotion, of these children, taking a violent part, and in such public questions, against both their parents, is not *in rerum natura*. Neither will it stand a moment's comparison with the history of the period. When Claverhouse was reducing the rebellious districts in 1682 (which he did without shedding a drop of blood), for a time he required every *adult* to show in the Established Church, that he might be able to distinguish the wolves from the flock. But at no time was it the inclination, or the system of the Restoration Governments to punish old or young for merely holding Covenanting opinions and being attached to the anti-prelatic form of church government and worship Conventicles were prohibited, and the preaching at them, and frequenting and following them was denounced, and endeavoured to be crushed by an impolitic *brutum fulmen* of legislation in 1670, that was never intended to be practically followed out. But these severe laws against conventicles were expressly levelled at them as " rendezvouses of rebellion," struggling to keep life in, and to revive the Dutch plot against the throne in 1666, and the Argyle regime of 1648 It was to meet that rebellious spirit, and those evil agitators in the kingdom, who accomplished in 1679 that brutal murder of the venerable Primate, over which Alexander Shields sang *Halleluja* and Wodrow chuckled with an ill-disguised delight. But a quiet Covenanter, taking care never to defy the law of the Government, and willing to absolve himself from all complicity with the Lynch-law of the Conventiclers, was as safe from Government prosecution as a loyalist. To pretend that the severe laws, passed from time to time as danger prompted, originated in an aristocratic design, or desire, to root out a conscientious and peaceable form of religion from among a saintly peasantry, or (to put it in Lord Macaulay's words) " to extirpate *Presbyterianism* by *drowning of women*, by the frightful torture of the boot," is neither history nor sense. Observe this fact, recorded by the *whig* Fountainhall :—" 12th November 1680—William Johnston and some other merchants were seized on upon a suspicion, but there being no evidence against them, further than that they were *strict Presbyterians*, they were *set at liberty.*" [1] And if this was the disposition of the Stuart Government as regards " strict Presbyterians," what could it have been towards a substantial farmer (and his young family of *daughters*) who was Conformist and Episcopalian " to ane excesse?" his wife being of the same persuasion, and peaceable habits? This question, too, we are able to illustrate from the Privy Council Records. On the 23d of January 1679,—" The Lords of his Majesty's Privy Council do hereby give order and warrant to the Bailies of Leith, to set at liberty furth of the Tolbooth of Leith, James Lawson, *a boy about the age of fourteen years*, prisoner there upon the account of conventicles " That a boy of that age, at such " rendezvouses of rebellion," might so demean himself as to get lodged in the Tolbooth of Leith, is perfectly intelligible. But the terms of that order can bear no other interpretation than that the Privy Council ordered his release on account of his youth. Again, on the 29th of May 1685, just seventeen days after the date of " that high-handed outrage by provincial agents," of whom *Lagg* is assumed to have been the leader, there appears in the register a letter, addressed by the Privy Council to *Viscount Kenmure* and *Sir Robert Grierson of Lagg*, as the leading Lords Commissioners for Wigtown and the Stewartry, empowering them to seize the horses and arms of suspected persons, in reference to the alarming crisis of Argyle's invasion. If that murderous mutiny, by Lagg, against the *humanity* of the Government to two insignificant women, had occurred seventeen days before, the news of it must by this time have reached the ears of the Privy Council, and could not fail to have created the greatest indignation and excitement. Some indication of this would

---

[1] Fountainhall's *Historical Observes*, p. 8

surely have appeared in the Privy Council instructions sent to that disturbed district. But what, on the 29th of the same month in which these women are said to have been thus *murdered*, is the tenor of the Government communication with the murderer, Lagg himself? Simply this composed and humane instruction, "*to report frequent accounts of your diligence, and of the condition of the place;*" to which orders this postscript is added—"*The Council doubt not but upon this occasion you will take care that honest men and their tenants meet with as little trouble as possible*"[1]

Well, then, if in the month of May 1685, the disposition of the Government was that Kenmure and Lagg were to "take care" that loyal and peaceable men and *their tenants* were to "meet with as little trouble as possible," could it possibly have been that such an *excessively* loyal tenant as Gilbert Wilson is said to have been, should, from the month of February of that same year, have been persecuted to his utter ruin, and his young and innocent children, some of them *mere infants*, and two of them *females*, hunted to the very death because they "would not conform!" Are we to believe that a girl of eighteen, taking along with her, from the nursery of her Episcopalian parents, a sister of thirteen, and a brother of sixteen, all with their infantine minds devoted to martyrdom, and sternly made up to the Presbyterian *dogma* and battle-word, that "Christ alone is King and Head of His Church" (meaning none but their own form of a Church), rushed from their well-conditioned home, "fled, and lived in the wild mountains, bogs, and caves" (which harboured the assassins of Archbishop Sharp, and the midnight murderers of the good minister of Carsphairn). until brought back by the violent exertions of an Executive deeply occupied at the time watching Argyle's invasion, to dungeons, and martyrdom or murder, the *loyal* Episcopalian parents being at the same time robbed by Government of all their great plenishing, and consigned to utter ruin? Are we to believe all that story in the face of human nature? In the face of common sense? In the face of unquestionable proof that the Government of that period

---

[1] Register of the Privy Council, 29th May 1685.

were mercifully inclined even towards the most violent and dangerous women; that children, even up to their *seventeenth year*, were *expressly exempt* from the penal laws against treasonable sedition; and that the Government waged no war even against *strict Presbyterians*, if they did not make common cause with rebellion, treason, and assassination? And what are we to say of the minister and Kirk-session of Penninghame, who gathered, prepared, recorded, attested, and sealed with prayer the most abominable nonsense that ever outraged the truth and justice of history? How are we to reconcile, even with itself, this *prepared statement* given in by the minister of Penninghame, when he tells us that this Episcopalian father was persecuted, on account of his children, "for *several years*," that he attended "the Court at Wigtown almost every week for *three years tyme*," on the subject, the persecution of the children having *commenced* in the month of February 1685, and been brought to its tragical *conclusion* on the 11th of May thereafter?

Nevertheless, it would seem, from the following passage in his Macmillan article, that the senior Principal of St Andrews desires to uphold those Kirk-Session Records for truth, and scorns the imputation of fiction! After narrating the whole story as if he thought it only a little "embellished," Dr Tulloch thus supports the record:—

"There is no evidence that the Kirk-Session Records of Penninghame and Kirkinner, Wodrow's authorities [1] (we do not need to *ascend farther*), are wilful fabrications, but every evidence to the contrary. The Records themselves appeal to living witnesses—among *others*, to a brother (Thomas) of Margaret Wilson—the young sufferer—who had borne arms 'under King William in Flanders and the Castle of Edinburgh,' and who was then, in 1711—only, after all, twenty-six years after the event—still living on *the remnants of the paternal acres* in Glenvernoch, [2] 'to certifie the truth of these things.' Besides, to those who know anything of the matter, it will seem next to impossible that such *documents* were *invented* The kirk-sessions of Penninghame and Kirkinner were composed of a

[1] The *Kirkinner* record is not alluded to by Wodrow, it was *contrasted* with the Penninghame record for the first time in "Memorials of Dundee"

[2] This is an amusing improvement by Dr Tulloch himself upon the Kirk-session record, which only gives us to understand that Thomas Wilson was dwelling upon the ground of his father's old farm. but too much reduced to take a farm himself

number of *grave and respected men*, who, whatever may have been their prejudices, would have shrunk from a falsehood with abhorrence. We are not bound to trust their judgment, nor even *reverence their faith*, but to suppose that these men wilfully imposed upon posterity *a fiction* (and if *the story* was *a fiction* they must have known it) is simply *incredible*."

But what, then, of the *Embellishments*, Doctor? What of your own previous admission, that "Wodrow's stories everywhere bear the stamp of *this imaginative development?*" For Wodrow got the whole of that story, *ipsissimis verbis*, in its fullest development, from that "grave and respected man," the minister of Penninghame. It is he who is answerable for all the embellishments. Do such embellishments, occasioned by "the imaginative fertility of the consciousness of the immediately succeeding time," not, in plain language, just mean *fiction?* And among the now *admitted* embellishments surrounding this martyrological romance, is it possible to avoid classing *the whole of that family history of the Wilsons?*

Equally incredible is the Session record of the trial and sentence. That the Lords Commissioners for Wigtonshire, of whom the *whig* Viscount Kenmure was *Convener*, did, under that special justiciary commission conferred upon Colonel Douglas,—(the instruction to which was that no female was to be tried or questioned who had not "been *active* in the said courses in a *signal* manner"),—serve a criminal libel upon a female child of *thirteen*, accusing her, in 1685, of being "guilty of the rebellion at Bothwell Bridge, Airdsmosse, twenty field conventicles, and twenty house conventicles," that the jury found her guilty, and that these Lords Commissioners condemned her to die, and in the face of the law, too, that the Oath of Abjuration could be tendered to none who were not "above the age of sixteen,"—of such a monstrous assertion as this surely we may say, that every unclouded mind must at once reject it with indignant contempt. Yet this is what was gathered, and given in to the Kirk-session of Penninghame by their minister, *attested for truth* by that clerical court, recorded *in perpetuam rei memoriam*, and sealed with prayer! What follows, by Dr Tulloch's own concession? Why, not only that these "grave and respected men" had recorded "a fiction," but the grossest fiction that ever insulted common sense; and that therefore, as the Principal decides, "they must have

known it." We do not call those *records* a " wilful fabrication."
We do not say that those " *documents* have been *invented*." But
we do say, that, from whatever source gathered, they *contain*
fabrications, and inventions, of the most ignorant stamp ; that
those clerical agitators, in their strong desire, and predeter-
mination, to get up a covenanting martyrology for Scotland,
had avoided all the proper sources of historical truth in such
matters ; that they had raked the gutters of fanaticism for
their facts ; and so, shutting their eyes to human nature, and
hardening their hearts against common sense, they did thereby
" wilfully impose upon posterity a fiction," involving a most
virulent calumny against James II. and his government of
Scotland.

What reliance, then, can be placed upon that " attestation
for truth," by the Kirk-session of Penninghame, and what is
the respect due to its clerical or religious character ? The
leading fact which it thus solemnly vouches, is, that these two
female martyrs were led forth to execution, and drowned, as
the *immediate* result of their trial and condemnation. That
this is what the Penninghame record means, and what was
understood by the minister, Robert Rowan, who gave the
extract to Wodrow, is also manifest from the fact, that Wodrow
himself so understood it, and so *narrated it in his History*,
until *better informed* by the Privy Council Register, which,
however, only induced him to add a garbled and deceptive
postcript. Now that story of an immediate execution is
proved to be false. What follows? The attestation of it by
the Kirk-session of Penninghame is false likewise.[1] Then,

---

[1] The parish minister, in giving out the extract to Wodrow, of the
sufferings of Penninghame, had taken the liberty to extract the *general
attestation* by the Session, in a form much more curt than it stands in the
original record, according to the Newton-Stewart print of it In Wodrow's manuscript it appears in this form —

" The above particulars being read in the Session of Penigham, the
twenty-fifth day of February 1711 years, are *attested to be true* by personal knowledge of many of them [*i. e.* many of *the particulars*], and by
incontestible information of *the rest*, except the particulars relative to
Gilbert Milroy after he was taken from Scotland, the truth whereof they
judge there is no ground to doubt

" Extracted by Rob Rowan, *Clk p t* "

—See " Memorials of Dundee," vol. ii. p 91.

besides that impossible story of the Government persecution of the *loyal* tenants, and hue and cry after the *infantine* rebels, they further attest for truth, that the female child of thirteen years of age was tried for high treason, by Lords Commissioners of Justiciary, and condemned to die. The very statement stamps this also as a falsehood. But its falsity can be proved by another strictly contemporaneous record of the same fanatical cast, to which we now turn.

Dr Tulloch, in repeating this family history of the Wilsons, and the trial and condemnation of the child, which he almost dares us to disbelieve, calls it "The *current tradition* of the story." That it was not a *tradition*, (in any proper understanding of that word) we have proved. All that nonsense was absolutely unknown in 1687. Neither was it ever *current* in the country. On the contrary, we proceed to show that, in 1714, even that vicious collection of sufferings, the "Cloud of Witnesses," tells another story altogether as to the persecution of the child of *thirteen*"

Wodrow's publication of the Wigtown romance in 1722, from the Penninghame Session-book of 1711,[1] was anticipated by an anonymous rival, or rivals, who published a rude collection of that same sort of calumnious rubbish in 1714, and gave it the title of "A Cloud of Witnesses for the Royal Prerogatives of Jesus Christ, or the last Speeches and Testimonies of those who have suffered for the Truth in Scotland, since the year 1680." In this we have the earliest *print* of the Wigtown martyrdom, wherein we find the falsehood assuming a different form, and in some respects *retrograding* from the embellish-

---

[1] In a fanatical History of Galloway, published by John Nicholson, at Kirkcudbright, in 1841, the Session-book of Penninghame is quoted, in illustration of the martyrdom in question, under this reckless assertion, —"We extract the following from the minutes of the kirk-session of Penninghame, *dated* 1685." This convenient mistake leads the unwary reader to suppose that the Penninghame record is *contemporaneous* with the alleged martyrdom. The true date is 1711 As this work, which is in two volumes, and crowded with notes and extracts, has an imposing air of research and authenticity, it was the more necessary to mark this dangerous blunder; which, however, we only impute to the ignorance of the covenanting compiler

ments of the Penninghame Session-book. Wodrow was jealous of this collection of sufferings, which appeared while he was busy with his history, and seemed to forestal him, and out-herod him, in its display of conventicle fanaticism In a letter to the London news-vender, George Ridpath (already mentioned), dated 3d September 1717, he thus notices the rival work :—" As to the speeches of our martyrs, I have indeed inserted none that are in *Naphtali*; that book is so common in this country, and has been so often printed, that I still referred to it; and we have another set of speeches printed lately by Mr M'Millan's people, all upon one side, in the *Cloud of Witnesses*, which, if you have seen, I doubt not you'll think *does neither that party nor us any service.*" [1] Nevertheless, Wodrow concocted his own version of the Wigtown martyrdom, with the Penninghame record in one hand and the " Cloud of Witnesses" in the other. What he did was this He squeezed out of the Cloud all that suited him; but when he found a statement, that tended to soften the savage character of the alleged persecution of the Wilson children, although that statement was, manifestly, a nearer approximation to truth, he rejected it in favour of the greater calumny of the kirk-session of Penninghame. In that earlier work the martyrdom is thus told, and entitled in the index, " A *Relation* concerning Margaret Lauchlane, and Margaret Wilson :"—

" Upon the 11th of May 1684,[2] Margaret Lauchlane, in the parish of Kirkkinner, and Margaret Wilson in Glenvernock, in the shire of Galloway, being sentenced to death for their non-compliance with Prelacy, and refusing to swear the oath of abjuration, by the Laird of Lagg, Captain Strachan, Colonel Mr David Graham, and Provost Cultron, who commanded them to receive their sentence upon their knees, which they refusing, were pressed down by force till they received it, and so were by their order tyed to a stake within the sea-mark, in the water of Blednoch, near Wigtoun, where, after they had made them wrestle long with the waves, which flowing, swelled on them by degrees. and had sometimes thrust them under water, and then pulled them out again, to see if

---

[1] " M'Millan's people " were a Presbyterian clique who took a somewhat wilder flight than Wodrow. He was jealous of them.

[2] The year is so given in every edition of " The Cloud of Witnesses." But from the sequence of dates in the collection, it would seem to be a stupid misprint for 1685

they would recant, they enduring death with undaunted courage, yielded up their spirits to God. The former was a widow woman of about sixty-three years, of a most Christian and blameless conversation, a pattern of piety and virtue, who having constantly refused to hear the curates, was much pursued and vexed, and at length taken by the soldiers, while she was devoutly worshipping God in her family, and being indicted of being at Bothwel-bridge, Airsmoss, and twenty field conventicles, and as many house conventicles, after sore and long imprisonment, without necessary refreshment of fire, bed, or diet, at length suffered this cruel death [1] The other (Margaret Wilson) a young woman of *scarce twenty-three years* of age, after she with her brother, who was about *nineteen*, and her sister *fifteen* years old, had been long driven from their father's house, and exposed to ly in dens and caves of the earth, wandering through the mosses and mountains of Carric, Nithsdale, and Galloway, going to Wigtoun secretly to visit the foresaid Margaret Lauchlane, was taken by the fraud of one Patrick Stewart, who under colour of friendship, having invited her and her sister to *drink with him*, offered them the king's health, and upon their refusal of it, as not warranted in God's Word, and contrary to *Christian moderation*, went presently out and informed against them *Her sister was dismissed, as being but fifteen years of age*, upon her father's paying a hundred pounds sterling for her ransom She [i e , Margaret] being examined whether she owned the king as head of the Church? and would take the abjuration oath? not answering to their pleasure, but adhering to the truth of Christ, was in like manner condemned, and after great severities of imprisonment, suffered the foresaid death Being put oft into the water, and when half-dead, taken up again, to see if she would take the oath, which she refused to her last breath, while her fellow-sufferers were wrestling with the waves, as being put first in to discourage her, the persecutors asked her, What she thought of that sight? She answered, 'What do I see but Christ (mystical) wrestling there?' One of the times that she was taken out of the water, they said, Say 'God save the king,' she returning with Christian meekness, I wish the salvation of all men, but the damnation of none. Upon which one of her friends, alledging she had said what they demanded, desired them to let her go But they would not, seeing she refused to take the oath During her imprisonment she wrote a large letter to her friends, wherein, besides the lively and feeling expression of God's love, she doth, with a judgment not usual for her age and education, disclose the unlawful nature of the abjuration oath, hearing of curates, owning the king's supremacy, which was a thing the per-

---

[1] It will be observed that it is only the old woman who is here said to have been accused of having been at Bothwell Bridge, Airsmoss, and forty conventicles. It is not pretended, in this version, that the young females were indicted for anything of the kind Yet the Penninghame kirk-session and Wodrow not only say so, but exclaim against the palpable falsity of the charge

secutors meant by his authority, and proves the necessity of her suffering upon these heads " [1]—*Cloud of Witnesses.*

Wodrow published his Penninghame version in 1722 There we have the interesting young *dramatis personæ,* described as " Thomas Wilson, a youth of *sixteen* years of age; Margaret Wilson, of *eighteen* years of age, and Agnes Wilson, a child *not thirteen* years." In " The Cloud of Witnesses," on the other hand, published in 1714, to which Wodrow repeatedly refers, and undoubtedly copied from, we have their ages stated thus:— " Margaret Wilson, a young woman of *scarce twenty-three* years of age, her brother about *nineteen,* and her sister *fifteen* years old." Was this authority for these ages not as good as the minister of Penninghame's? Did this not look a little more like the truth? It was, probably, more the " current story" that Dr Tulloch speaks of, than the other version. Why, then, did Wodrow reject it? For the same reason that Lord Macaulay (who quotes the " Cloud") ignored it The Penninghame version, however false, was a better martyrological calumny against James II. and his government of Scotland.

But the disingenuousness of Wodrow shows more palpably in his assertion of *Agnes* Wilson having been indicted, remitted to a jury, found guilty of high treason, and condemned to be drowned. " No matter now," he exclaims with holy indignation, " how false and calumnious poor people's *indictments* were; *Agnes* Wilson could be but eight years of age at *Ausmosse; all the three* refused the Abjuration Oath; it was *unaccountable* it should be put to one of them; the assize bring them in guilty; the Judges pronounce their sentence, that, upon the 11th *instant* all *the three* should be tied to stakes fixed within the flood-mark, in the water of Blednoch, near Wigtown, where the sea flows at high-water, there to be drowned. We *have seen* that *Agnes* Wilson was got out by

---

[1] Compare this last paragraph with the same in Wodrow,—see before, p. 11. The martyrologist had, manifestly, just copied it out of " The Cloud of Witnesses," with a little cunning transposition of the expressions, and knew no more about the matter. No such statement occurs in the Penninghame Session-book This proves that Wodrow had " The Cloud of Witnesses " in his hand while concocting his romance

her father upon a bond of an hundred pounds *sterling*, which, *I hear*, upon her *non-production* was likewise *exacted*.' [1] But Wodrow had seen something else than this. He had seen, from "The Cloud of Witnesses," published eight years before, that soon after the alleged apprehension of the two wandering sisters, *Agnes* " was *dismissed* as being but *fifteen* years of age, upon her father's paying a hundred pounds *sterling* for her ransom." That is a totally different story. But even here we have the most palpable falsehood that was ever penned, mixed up with a reflected light from the truth It was the law, a law never in a single instance departed from, that the test of the Abjuration Oath was only to be applied to such as were *above the age of sixteen*. Of course, the child of fifteen was *dismissed*. We don't believe she was apprehended. But that very law implied that any *ransom* was out of the question, and that the enormous ransom of a hundred pounds *sterling* (of which no official record exists) was exacted in 1685 from a loyal father relative to the humane fact of his female child being " dismissed *as being* but fifteen years of age," is a specimen of stupid, blundering inconsistency, which the Head of St Mary's may call a natural embellishment if he please, but which common sense must at once refer to a gross and ignorant spirit of falsehood. Yet it was not false enough for Wodrow. He preferred the falsehood as recorded and attested by the Kirk-session of Penninghame.

In 1717, still ere the illustrious Wodrow occupies the field, another anonymous collection of sufferings appeared, absurdly entitled, "Memoirs of the Church of Scotland, in Four Periods " It was written by De Foe, and therefore may be treated tenderly. Had Wodrow ever proved himself so *splendide mendax* as the author of *Robinson Crusoe*, he might have been forgiven his " Sufferings of the Kirk " It seems to have occurred to Crusoe, that the Cloud of Witnesses had not made enough of the old woman in the story. So he invents a grand martyrological duet between the sufferers, which being duly performed,

---

[1] But if this child, not thirteen, had been " got out " after trial and condemnation to death, what was she to be *reproduced* for? To be drowned? A hundred pounds sterling was a very large sum in 1685

I

he then ties them to the *same* stake, and, without more ado, drowns them together, the " young maiden of *eighteen*" acquiring in his hands additional interest from being " about *sixteen* years old."

" The first I meet with is the story of a poor woman and a young maiden of about *sixteen* years old, in the West of Scotland, who were cruelly murdered by *some men belonging to* Grierson of Log, an eminent persecutor in that part of the country. They began by putting the questions to them above mentioned, and the first they offered, as what was most *popular* at that time in the world, and best served, as they thought, to expose the persecuted to the Court, was that of, ' *Will ye say God bless the King.*' As I have received this story from *creditable* witnesses, take it as follows —

" The *woman* told them she should pray to God to forgive the King his sins. The *maid* said, she would pray that God would please to give the King repentance ' But it would be an *impious* thing,' said the *woman*, ' to pray to God to save, that is to bless, a Covenant-breaking, perjured *magistrate*, and in the prosecution of his perjury too ,' and they both declared it was against their consciences, their principles, and the Covenant, and that therefore they would not do it The *woman* said boldly, that while the King was a persecutor of God's people he was an enemy to God, and to the church of God ; and she thought it was an abominable thing to ask of any Christian to pray to God for prosperity to the persecutors of the Church of Christ ; for that was to say *God speed to them*, even in the very persecution itself She was an *undaunted* woman, and challenged them to answer her in that particular But they had nothing to say to her argument, but thought she would have some regard to theirs, which was,—*Pray to God to bless the King—or die* ' Will ye kill me,' says the *woman*, ' because I will not bless those who God curses ? The Lord forbid that I should do it, though I were to die a thousand times ' *Upon this* they fixed a stake in the sea, at the low water-mark, and *binding the poor woman and the young girl to the stake*, let them stand there till the tide flowed over them and drowned them both , being also *tormented almost to death by the cold*,[1] by standing in the water so long as till the tide was high enough to drown them However, they both endured it with great constancy, and without the least offer of compliance with the barbarous adversary "

Then comes Patrick the Pedler, beating even Robinson Crusoe in graphic power and vigour of dialogue. Moreover, Patrick had no idea of the ogre *Lagg* coming off so cheaply,

---

[1] This artistic touch of *vraisemblance* is very characteristic of the author of Robinson Crusoe. Manifestly, what he describes is the scene at a *trial*, not at an *execution* De Foe's version was entirely ignored, until quoted in " Memorials of Dundee "

as this reference of the murder to " some men *belonging to Grierson of Log* " enabled him to do. And so, in 1727, five years after Wodrow, we have, from a stall in the West-port of Auld Reekie, the fanatical Chapman's tract, which may be called the cheap cursing and swearing edition for the people

" The broth was *hell-hot* in these days; they *wanted long-shanked spoons that supped with the devil.* I could give *many* instances, but at this time shall only mention the drowning of these two women at Wigtown, the 11th of May 1685 (*which some deny to be matter of fact*), viz, *Margaret Lachlan,* who was past *sixty-three* years, and some of her intimates said to me, she was a Christian of deep exercise through much of her life, and of high attainments and great experiences in the ways of godliness, and *Margaret Wilson,* who was put to death with her, aged *twenty-three* The old woman was first tied to the stake, enemies saying,—' *Tis needless to speak to that old damned bitch, let her go to Hell* ' ' But,' say they, ' *Margaret, ye are young,* if ye'll *pray for the King we will give you your life.*' She said,—' *I'll pray for the salvation of all the elect, but the damnation of none.*' They dashed her under the water, and pulled her up again. People looking on said,—' O, Margaret, *will ye say it?*' She said,—' *Lord give him repentance, forgiveness, and salvation, if it be Thy holy will*' Lagg cried,—' *Damned bitch, we don't want such prayers, tender the oaths to her*' She said,—' *No, no sinful oaths for me*' They said,—' *To Hell with them, to Hell with them, it is o'er good for them*' Thus suffered they that extraordinary and unheard of death " [1]

We recommend the study of this crowning version of the martyrdom to Dr Tulloch, as affording by far the best illustration of his ingenious theory, that " the *imaginative fertility* of the consciousness of the immediately succeeding time, learns to look back with a *reverend wonder* and *love* to the tragic events which made *heroic* [2] the former days." And is the conscious-

---

[1] Patrick Walker's " Vindication of Mr Cameron's name," originally printed as a chapman's tract, and reprinted in *Presbyteriana Scotica*, 1827.

[2] The *heroism* of the former days is curiously illustrated by the Whig Fountainhall's record of the death of the conventicle apostle Cargill — " They all died a great deal more stout and firm than their leader *Cargill,* who behaved *most timerously to save his life* (if it could have been converted to banishment), and *minched their principles,* and *begged for a longer time,* that he might be judged in Parliament, but finding there was no remedy, he put on more staidness and resolution after his sentence."—*Historical Observes,* p 45 The heroism of the former days also sometimes smelt of brandy. Those conventicle ranters, Kidd and King, were hanged in the Grassmarket on the 14th August 1679, for their share in Bothwell Bridge " They died," says Wodrow in 1722, " in full

ness of the succeeding time, or times, always to look back in
the vein of " imaginative fertility," and never in the spirit of
truth and justice?   How came Walker to *omit the reprieve*,
noticed by Wodrow *five years before?*   Is the Hind Let Loose
in the seventeenth century still to ride rough-shod over History
from her lair, or her chair, in the nineteenth century?   In
reference to the most necessary system of scattering the armed
conventicles, and pursuing broken bands of outlawed rebels, and
endeavouring to apprehend those conventicle preachers,—who,
as Patrick Walker boasts, " came to the west of Scotland in
order to *engage, preach up*, and *prepare a people to join Argyle*,"
—Dr Tulloch has the following passage, by way of make-weight
against the proofs collected in " Memorials of Dundee " for
the more laudable purpose of destroying such calumnies

" But the *excesses* of the Government, or of its agents, were systematic
and *cold-blooded* to a degree that stirs one with *detestation* after the lapse
of nearly two centuries   Parties of soldiers hunted *poor wretches* for days
over wild moorland tracts, their *only crime* being that they *would not
attend the Episcopal service* ('), and when they startled them from their
lair in the dank heather, and surrounded them, famished, and half-
maniacal, with their long privations, *shot them down remorselessly without
giving them time even to murmur a prayer* "

Mighty fine this, but all false.   *C'est magnifique, mais ce
n'est pas l'Histoire.*   And how is it possible to attach any
weight to Dr Tulloch's own argument, that " the Kirk-sessions of Penninghame and Kirkinner were composed of grave
and respected men, who, whatever may have been their
prejudices, would have shrunk from a falsehood with abhorrence,"—when we find, in the year 1862, the grave and
respected Senior Principal of the University of St Andrews
indulging in this old clap-trap of mythical facts, and mouldy
pathos, in order to make a case of savage cruelty against the

peace, serenity, and joy."   But Fountainhall, the usual Whig counsel for
such criminals, and who most probably witnessed their execution, tells
us,—" Many thought Kid more composed than Mr King, and some ad-
ventured to say, that Mr King, for *infusing courage into him*, had drunk
more than was fit for him to do, which,"—adds the Whig jurisconsult,
as if no way doubting the fact,—" is a *most dangerous practice* "—(*Historical Notices*, vol. i p 229)   Their treason was Dutch, and their
courage was in keeping with it

governments of the Restoration, which he could no more prove than he could have written Gulliver's Travels, or Robinson Crusoe? We have here language as violent, and a calumny as baseless, as if it had emanated from Alexander Shields, or Patrick the Pedler. Dr Tulloch is the less excuseable, seeing he had before him, in the very work he affects to treat as worthless, abundant materials for disproving that statement. The great leader in those scenes he so falsely describes, was Claverhouse. How they were conducted, why, and with what success, is now fully illustrated by his own admirable letters, reports, and despatches, all published in " Memorials of Dundee." Nothing of the kind can be more interesting than the true light thus thrown by Claverhouse himself upon all those military and executive operations. With a conventicle he never came into shooting collision at all, except upon one single occasion, and that was at *Drumclog*, where he was defeated with great loss, and was very nearly sacrificed himself. At that conventicle the leading assassins of the venerable Primate, were commanding. That conventicle carried the bloody banner of " no quarter.' Upon one other occasion, Claverhouse caught the murderous rebels he was pursuing, an incident which is thus recorded by the whig Fountainhall :—

" 20th December 1684 —Letters came from Colonel Graham of Claverhouse, then in Galloway, that he had met with a party of these rogues, who had skulked in the mountains,—if their retiring holes could be got, they are so *cowardly* they may be easily routed,—he had followed them, killed five, and taken three prisoners, some of which were of the *murderers of the minister of Carsphairn*, and that he was to judge and execute the three prisoners by his Justiciary power, and if his *garrisons* were once placed, he hoped to *secure and quiet the country*" [1]

Now the fugitives thus vigorously, and most justly dealt with, were part of a band of armed outlaws, who, after murdering the minister of Carsphairn, had increased to the number of a hundred and eight, attacked the town of Kirkcudbright, stormed the tolbooth, released the prisoners, killed the sentinel, and carried off the town-drum, and all the arms they

---

[1] This notice by Fountainhall is the more valuable, that we could not discover, among the Queensberry Papers, the letters of Claverhouse to which it refers

could find. But, generally speaking, these hill-rebels were *never caught*, and the troops were worn out, and harassed to death in fruitless pursuit of them. Of this, Claverhouse continually complains, in letters of graphic power. And such scenes, as the ruthless massacre of "poor wretches whose only crime was that they would not attend the Episcopal service," as described by Dr Tulloch, never occurred, in a single instance, under the leadership of Claverhouse, Lord Ross, Colonel Douglas, or any other officer, during the whole period of the Restoration.[1]

SECTION IX

The Tomb-stones and Epitaphs.

Had that melo-dramatic martyrdom really occurred at Wigtown, it must have been followed, immediately, by a closing scene scarcely less exciting. That those minute and graphic reminiscences of such a *death* could exist so vividly in 1710, as a true tradition, and no reminiscence whatever remain of the *burial*, is impossible. The lifeless bodies of these interesting and dearly beloved martyrs, surrounded as they were in their last agonies by their own relations (as the story goes), and by hundreds, if not thousands, of a sympathising people, must have attracted the tenderest care of a multitude of heart-wrung mourners, whenever the tide retired, and gave up the tenantless clay. But not a word did the ministers of Kirkinner and Penninghame gather regarding either the scene or the place of their interment. Of all that multitude, and all those relations who must have wept bitterly at the closing scene, were there none in 1710, twenty-five years after the event, to point

---

[1] Colonel Douglas also made a very narrow escape in pursuing some of these ruffians " January 1685 —Colonel James Douglas being one day in the fields in Galloway, with a small party of eight or ten, he meets with as many of the rebels at a house, who *kill two of his men*, and *Captain Urquhart*, Meldrum's brother , and had very nearly *shot Douglas himself dead*, had not the whig's carabine misgiven ; whereupon Douglas pistolled him presently. Urquhart is the only staff-officer this *desperate crew* have yet had the honour to kill "—*Fountainhall*

out precisely where they were laid? Whoever remained, not one, not even Thomas Wilson, said to be alive in 1710, and "ready to certify" all the rest, had furnished these kirk-sessions with a single trait of the interment, or a precise idea of its locality. These ministers, so deeply interested to place such a story of suffering beyond the reach of doubt or cavil, had gathered not a word on the subject. And, accordingly, neither the "Relation" in the "Cloud of Witnesses," nor De Foe, nor Wodrow, nor Walker, speak of their interment, or tell us distinctly where they lie. The actual spot is left, to this day, as uncertain as the grave of Moses.

Yet surely the closing scene, if not so harrowing, must have been as solemn, as awful, as heart-rending, and attended by as many hundreds of weeping witnesses, as that which preceded it. How comes it that no tradition of that scene "has lived universally in the hearts of the peasantry in Galloway since the commencement of last century?" Because *the women were not drowned*. What! says Dr Tulloch, "were the two women never *at all* drowned at Wigtown? And Wodrow, and *Macaulay* after him, and the Kirk-session Records of Penninghame, and the *old stone* in the grave-yard of Wigtown parish-church,—are they *all* pure romances—some of them much worse than this?" Yes, Doctor, yes, even so. We condole with you. There is pathos in that expiring cry of a long cherished calumny, "a beautiful old story." But even the "old stone," which we now proceed to consider, tells nothing but the falsehood that had been told before.

The first reference to the fact that these martyrs were allowed a grave other than the sand of the Solway, is to be found in the "Cloud of Witnesses," but not in its "Relation" of the Martyrdom. At the conclusion of that volume, an Appendix of Epitaphs is thus modestly introduced to the public by "M'Millan's people," in 1714.[1]

---

[1] We here assume that the epitaph to *Margaret Wilson*, which appears in the later editions of the Cloud of Witnesses, was also published in the original edition 1714. But we have been able to discover only two copies of that original edition, and in both of them the appendix of epitaphs at the end happens to be imperfect. It is of little consequence, however, as regards proof of the martyrdom

"The *Epitaphs*, or *Inscriptions*, upon the Tombs or Grave-stones of the Martyrs, in several Church-yards, and other places where they ly buried The reader is desired to remember, that they, *being mostly composed by illiterate country people*, one cannot reasonably expect neatness and elegant poetry in them, and therefore will readily pardon any harshness in the phrase, or metre, which he may meet with"

This apology looks very much as if the *Epitaphs* had all been written for the collection in which they are published. But we shall approach the literary study of them in a frame of the critical mind far more humble and forbearing than that displayed by some of "M'Millan's people" in our own time. Among many other specimens of this illiterate muse, crowned with hemlock and nettles, appears the following:—

"Upon a stone in the Church-yard of Wigtown, on the body of Margaret Wilson, who was drowned in the water of Blednoch, upon the 11th of May, 1684 [*sic*], by the laird of Lagg, &c.

'Let earth and stone still witness bear,
There lyes a virgin Martyr here
Murder'd for owning Christ supreme,
Head of his Church, and no more crime,
But her not owning Prelacy,
And not abjuring Presbytery.
Within the sea, ty'd to a stake,
She suffered for Christ Jesus sake
The actors of this cruel crime
Was Lagg, Winram, Strachan, and Graham
Neither young years, nor yet old age,
Could quench the fury of their rage'"

This "old stone," which Lord Macaulay also thought worth quoting, (and quoted wrong), Principal Tulloch seizes as a starving man would an old bone. "A memorial," he says, "in the churchyard of Wigtown, as old as 1714, commemorates the drowned 'martyrs.' The *antiquity* of this memorial does not *admit of question* (!) Even if the stone should have been *renewed*, there was *evidently* a memorial of some standing in 1714." *Quomodo constat*, Doctor? In the first place, it only professes to commemorate one of the martyrs. Again, this falsehood having been recorded, *in extenso*, in the Penninghame Session-book in 1711, an *epitome* of it, in the form of an epitaph, composed by some of the "illiterate country people," appearing in such a work as the "Cloud of Witnesses," published in 1714, was just what might be expected, and affords no proof whatever of the martyrdom. It by no means even absolutely proves that those lines were actually inscribed on a tomb-stone at the time of the publication. They may only have been composed at that time, for that purpose. In Sir John Sinclair's statistical account of the parish of Dunkeld, in reference to a church-yard there, it is stated,—" One epitaph should be mentioned, which has been *frequently repeated as copied from a tomb-stone there.* But, though it was composed on the person to whom it relates, and who was an inhabitant of Dunkeld, it was *never actually inscribed.* Her name was Marjory Scot. One of her descendants is still alive, who recollects to have seen her, and reports that it was composed by Mr Pennycook She died in 1728." Now this is far more likely to have happened as regards the voluminous collection of martyr epitaphs at the end of the Cloud of Witnesses, most of which appear to have issued from the same mint. But the question is of little importance, as it has never been pretended that any epitaph, upon either of these women, or any record of their interment in Wigtown church-yard, existed prior to the Revolution. This, too, is remarkable, that in the collection of 1714 there is no epitaph on old Margaret Lauchlison. Surely if they perished together at Wigtown in the manner narrated, they would not be separated in death. And was old Saint Margaret not as worthy of an epitaph as the young saint? Although this hemlock poet had neglected her, however, more modern records have assigned old Margaret Lauchlison a grave in Wigtown church-yard also, and a stone, if not to mark the spot, at least to assert the fact The following is from the fanatical History of Galloway, 1841 ·—

"These female martyrs were interred in Wigtown church-yard ; a stone, with this inscription, is *in the wall of the church*

"'Here lyes Margaret Lachlane, who was by unjust law sentenced to die by Lagg, Strachan, Winrame, and Grame, and tyed to a stake within the flood for her adherence to Scotland's Reformation, Covenants, National and Solemn League, Aged 63 1685.

"'Here lyes Margaret Wilson, daughter to Gilbert Wilson in Glenvernoch, who was drowned, anno 1685 '

"' Let earth and stone still witness bear,
There lyes a virgine martyre here,
Murther'd for owning Christ supreme,
Head of his Church and no more crime,

But not abjuring Presbytery,
And her not owning Prelacy.
They her condemned by unjust law,
Of Heaven nor Hell they stood no awe
Within the sea tyed to a stake,
She suffered for Christ Jesus sake
The actors of this cruel crime
Was Lagg, Strachan, Winram and Grahame
Neither young years, nor yet old age,
Could stop the fury of their rage.' "

Here the stone is said to be in the wall of the church; and the metrical inscription is not precisely the same as that published in 1714. The fifth and sixth lines are transposed, and the seventh and eighth lines are interpolated. Had Old Mortality been at work? Again, in the Reverend Mr Anderson's "Ladies of the Covenant," we have it thus boldly recorded, in another form:—

"The bodies of the two martyrs, on being taken from the waters, were buried in the churchyard of Wigtown A stone was afterwards erected to their memory. The particular date of its erection cannot now be ascertained, but, from the freedom of its language, it is evident that it was *after the Revolution*. It is placed *in the wall of the church*, and the inscription upon it, copied *verbatim et literatim*, is as follows:—

HERE LIES MARGARAT LACHLANE
WHO WAS BY UNJUST LAW SENTENCED
TO DYE BY LAGG STRACHANE WINRAME
AND GRAME AND TYED TO A STAKE WITH
IN THE FLOOD FOR HER *
      ME MENTO MORI

SURNAMED GRIER

* ADHERENCE TO SCOTLAND'S REFORMATION
COVENANTS NATIONAL AND SOLEMN LEAGUE
AGED 63   1685.

HERE LYES MARGRAT WILSON
DOUGHTER TO GILBLET WILSON
IN GLENVERNOCH WHO WAS
DROUND ANNO 1685
AGED 18

LET EARTH AND STONE STILL WITNESS BEARE
THEIR LYES A VIRGINE MARTYR HERE
MURTHERD FOR OWNING CHRIST SUPREME,
HEAD OF HIS CHURCH AND NO MORE CRIME
BUT NOT ABJURING PRESBYTERY,
AND HER NOT OWNING PRELACY,
THEY HER CONDEMND, BY UNJUST LAW,
OF HEAVEN NOR HELL THEY STOOD NO AW
WITHIN THE SEA TYD TO A STAKE;
SHE SUFFERED FOR CHRIST JESUS SAKE
THE ACTORS OF THIS CRUEL CRIME
WAS LAGG, STRACHAN WINRAM AND GRAHAME
NEITHER YOUNG YEARS, NOR YET OLD AGE
COULD STOP THE FURY OF THERE RAGE.

Whether these be accurate transcripts, as they profess to be, we cannot tell from personal inspection. Certainly this last is not the stone of 1714; for the "Cloud of Witnesses" states the age of Margaret Wilson to be "*scarce twenty-three years.*" As we are not fortified either with the courage, or the grey mare of Tam o' Shanter, we think it best, under all the circumstances, not to venture into the churchyard of Wigtown, where haply the two Margarets' ghosts still walk. Whatever the condition of the old stone, or stones, whether in the wall of the church, or on the ground, they can add not one iota of proof in support of the martyrdom, nor detract in the slightest degree from the proof against it. They are at best an illiterate epitome, on stone, of a more detailed calumny recorded in the Kirk-session books of the eighteenth century.

The obscure condition (in their own time) of these poor women, and the imperfect condition of the parish registers of Scotland, especially as regards obituaries, have combined to baffle all our researches on the subject of their actual fate. We believe them to be dead now; and humbly trust they are in possession of brighter crowns of glory than they could ever gain from a fanaticism that was utterly devoid of the true spirit of Christianity. To destroy the false legend of their martyrdom is surely good service to a most important chapter of the History of Scotland, that has never yet been truly written by our greatest historians. Bishop Russell, in his excellent and most temperate "History of the Church in Scotland," justly observes :—" In the conduct of the rigid Covenanters, there is nothing more remarkable than their disposition to *slander*, and the *reckless intrepidity* with which they scattered around them the most *atrocious calumnies*"—(Vol. II. p. 264.) *Ex uno disce omnes.*

Neither martyrdoms, nor religious persecution, can be truly and justly laid to the charge of the Restoration governments. The throne had to be defended against internal rebellion going hand in hand with foreign invasion. That a pious and peaceable people in Scotland were driven into acts of violence and wickedness by cruelty and oppression, is the usual apology for the obstinate and desperate struggles of the rump of the Argyle regime, to regain the most vicious rule under which

Scotland ever suffered. But that threadbare excuse cannot be verified by a single well vouched illustration. Good men may become martyrs under oppression, but never rendered murderers and cowardly assassins. Charles the Second signed the Covenants, and was crowned by Argyle. Charles the Second burnt the Covenants, and beheaded Argyle. Montrose would have told him, *and did tell him*, by that dishonest dealing with, and recognition of, your worst enemies, your father's murderers, you are disgracing yourself as a man and a Christian, and dethroning yourself as a monarch. The penalty was exacted in the Conventicle rebellion, and the Dutch invasion. But the Privy Council records of Scotland, those very records which Wodrow so dishonestly handled, of themselves suffice to bear witness, that, under the most critical circumstances for the Monarchy, and the most intense provocation to the Executive, the Governments of the Restoration never lost sight of the principle of humanity, and never failed to exercise forbearance, whenever that was consistent with a due regard to the lives of the lieges, and of the Sovereign, the suppression of traitorous and murderous plots, and the standing of the Throne. It was the desperate violence and wickedness of these plotters, and the ceaseless truculent agitations of the conventicle leaders, that occasioned the severities of Government, and called forth at times that lamentable law of the criminal code—a law far more shamefully exercised by King William and his minister Hamilton, after the Revolution, —the law of judicial torture. These, and *never* the innocent or religious, were the objects of Government pursuit, and Government retribution. No female rebel suffered death by drowning in either reign. Two suffered death on the gallows in the reign of Charles II., and compelled their own fate. Under the regime of Argyle and the Kirk, *eighty helpless women and children* were cast over Linlithgow bridge, at one time, and *six more* at Elgin, drowned and massacred by the very sect who, in the succeeding reign, raised the false cry of cruelty.[1]

---

[1] This horrible massacre is proved beyond question by other contemporaneous evidence, besides the statement by Sir George Mackenzie, in his " Vindication," which his Cameronian opponent did not contradict

What zealots have recorded those poor Irish mothers and their infants as martyrs? Who have erected monuments to that wholesale sacrifice?—an awful tale of remorseless murder—a tale, alas! too true.[1] It is not the morbid, misdirected fervour of religion, falsely so called, the sordid bigotry, or the redundant use, and the grotesque abuse, of scriptural phraseology, that will suffice to characterise the whig-fanatics of Scotland. The climax and corner-stone of the character, is their sanguinary violence, not merely in defence of their own tenets and discipline, but in forcing the same upon all others, *vi et armis;* their tendency to outrage, in their ever aggressive obstinacy, all laws human and divine, their disregard even of the *semblance* of truth, in their deadly vituperations, and that vile system, arising out of such disorganisation of legitimate government, whereby every man may claim a divine mission to judge, and to execute judgment upon, his neighbour who opposes or offends him. Alas! the crimson vein of the Kirk's Lynch-law, may be too distinctly traced, running on, through all the various formations and strata of the Church as *reformed* in Scotland; and the in-

---

[1] The contemporary chronicler, Patrick Gordon, speaks of the prisoners who were " murthered by the way at *Lithgoe* "—(*Britane's Distemper,* p. 160.) This corroborates Mackenzie Leslie's line of march from Philiphaugh to Glasgow was by Linlithgow Wishart records, " that there was a most cruel butchery of what prisoners the rebels had, without any distinction of sex or age, some falling into the hands of the country people were basely murthered by them; others who escaped them (and found some pity in them who had so little) were, by orders from the rebel lords, *thrown headlong from off a high bridge,* and the men, together with their *wives* and *sucking children,* drowned in the river beneath; and if any chanced to swim towards the side, they were beaten off with pikes and staves, and thrust down again into the water."—(*Contemporary Translation,* 1648) This also corroborates Mackenzie, who gives the precise number of innocent women and children thus butchered in cold blood. David Leslie was attended by a staff of " gracious ministers." The picture is awfully darkened by the fact, that the Bible was perverted to enforce these murders. " Thine eye shall not pity, and thou shalt not spare,"—and,—" what meaneth then this bleating of the sheep in my ears, and the lowing of the oxen,"—were the texts by which, upon this and other occasions, the Covenanting preachers diverted from defenceless prisoners the rude mercies of soldiers weary of blood.

stances are but too many and conspicuous, in which the worst
of murderers, assuming for their own savage ends the most
sanctified garb of the sect, have been by them received as
brothers, and their services acknowledged with scarcely disguised satisfaction and gratitude.

When Magus Moor sent forth a suppliant cry,
A daughter's writhing form was interposed ,
But the sword stay'd not   the fell caitiffs closed,
    And the Kirk kept her ancient cruelty
How little boots that fair girl's fortitude,
    Wounded and trod on, thou canst testify,
For Scotland's shame, O Magus Moor ! where blood,
    And scatter'd brains, invoke the vengeful sky
To launch its lightnings on the Covenant
    Foul murder ! done by those who dare to draw,
E'en from the Book of Life, intolerant
    Death-warrants ' Bishops bleed by Hell's lynch-law,
    But who would slay the Church, tilts with a straw,
Against a champion cased in adamant

THE END.

PRINTED BY JOHN HUGHES, 3 THISTLE STREET

CPSIA information can be obtained at www.ICGtesting.com
Printed in the USA
LVOW022306230413

330523LV00010B/401/P